BURIAL HILL

EARLY STORIES IN STONE

LEXI MYERS

AMERICA
—
THROUGH
—
TIME

To my kids, I hope you always follow whatever interests you and fills your heart, even the strange and unusual.

Aᴍᴇʀɪᴄᴀ Tʜʀᴏᴜɢʜ Tɪᴍᴇ®
An imprint of Sᴜᴛᴛᴏɴ Pᴜʙʟɪsʜɪɴɢ ɪɴᴄ
www.through-time.com

First published 2025

Copyright © Lexi Myers 2025

ISBN 978-1-63499-514-6

Typeset in 10pt on13pt Sabon
Printed and bound in England

Contents

Acknowledgments 4

1 After Plymouth Rock: Historical Context 5

2 Historical Graves: Notable Names 31

3 Families of Plymouth 40

4 Early Colonial Life in Massachusetts 62

5 Unique Headstones 80

References 94

About the Author 96

$\mathcal{A}$CKNOWLEDGMENTS

Special thanks to Diane Maguire and Connor Anderson for coordinating with me on this project. Additionally, thank you to my friend, Brian, for his help.

1

After Plymouth Rock: Historical Context

Burial Hill in Plymouth, MA, is the second oldest cemetery in the town. The first cemetery was Coles Hill, though there are no grave markers there today. It is also hard to say when burials began on Burial Hill for the same reason: grave markers back then were made from wood. You'll be able to see throughout this book how the stone markers are breaking apart, so you can imagine what happened to the wood after so long.

When we learn about history, we are often hit with the phrase, "Times were different." It is easy to forget how things used to be for many, with their day-to-day lives looking much different than ours. You don't need to go far in an old cemetery to discover those differences.

Parents often outlived their children. I have come across several families with multiple children with the same name. It was common for children to die young and their parents to name their subsequent child the same. I'm not sure if this was a Pilgrim practice or maybe more common in the Northeast, as I have yet to see this name trend in the South.

There was rampant disease, war, and men lost at sea. There's a mass grave in this cemetery, but then there is also the opposite: empty graves with just a tombstone to mark remembrance for the man lost to the sea. Of the cemeteries I have visited, Plymouth has been the one with the most empty graves that I've noticed, with tombstones put up only in that person's memory rather than to mark their grave.

There are plain graves, intricate graves, and some crumbling to time. There are governors, congressmen, and ship captains. There are also many stories of everyday people. And while it would take years to properly document each of the over 2,000 graves in the cemetery, it is important to share what we can find so that all stories are remembered.

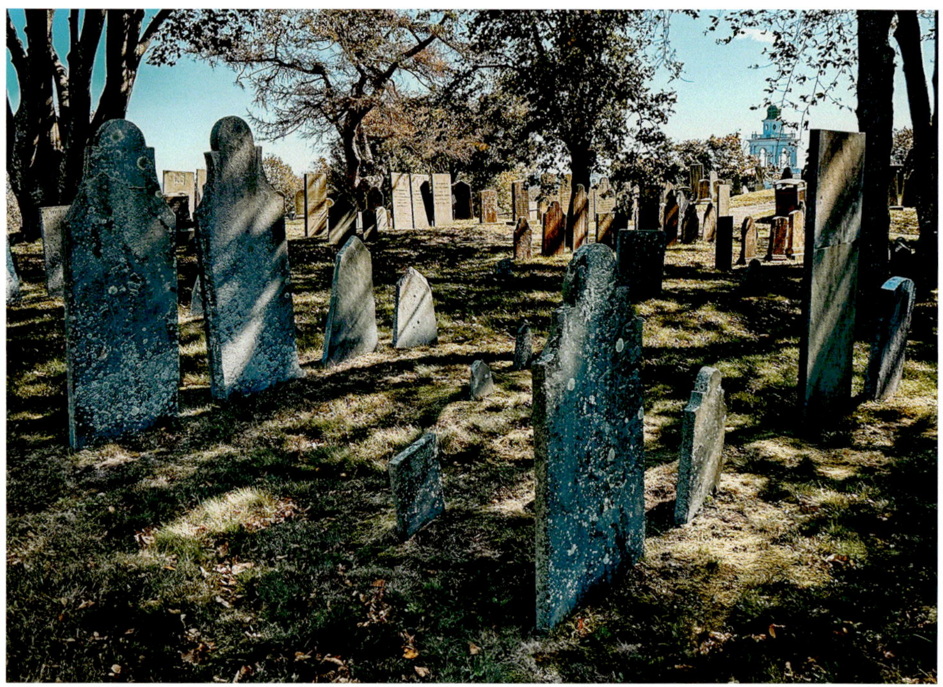

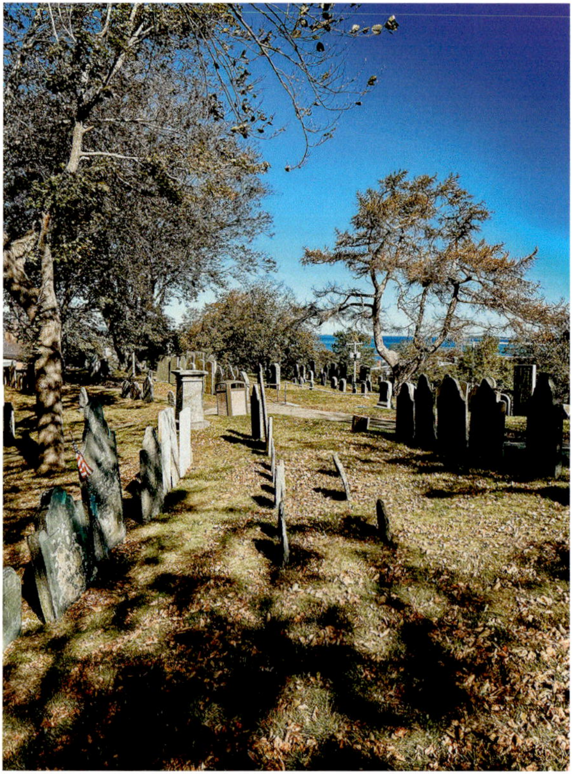

Above: After my first visit to Plymouth in 2015, I fell in love and couldn't wait to go back. It took some time, but I got back there in the fall of 2023. The photos in this book are all from that trip, when I visited the cemetery with just my camera.

Left: Burial Hill is the ideal place to visit for those that love history.

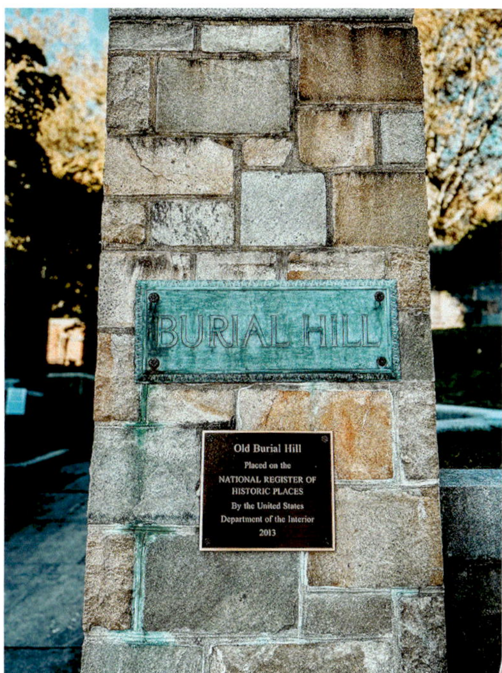

Right: A sign at the entrance to
Old Burial Hill, notating that it
is on the National Register of
Historic Places as of 2013.

Below: Burial Hill is a cemetery
that quickly captured my heart with
its beautiful and peaceful setting.

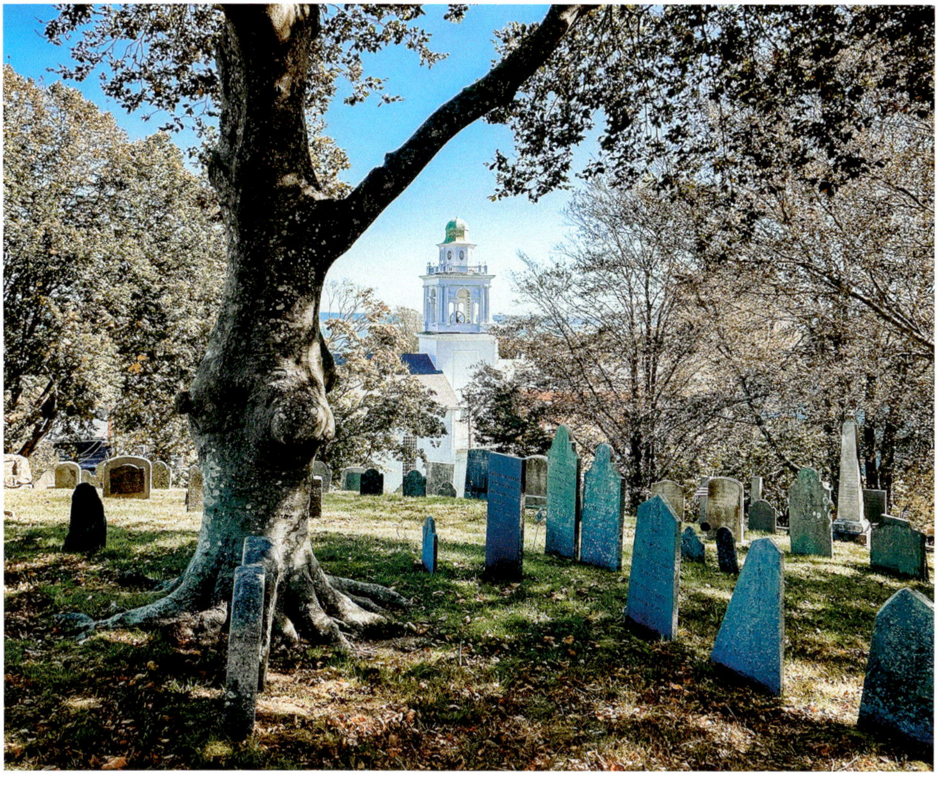

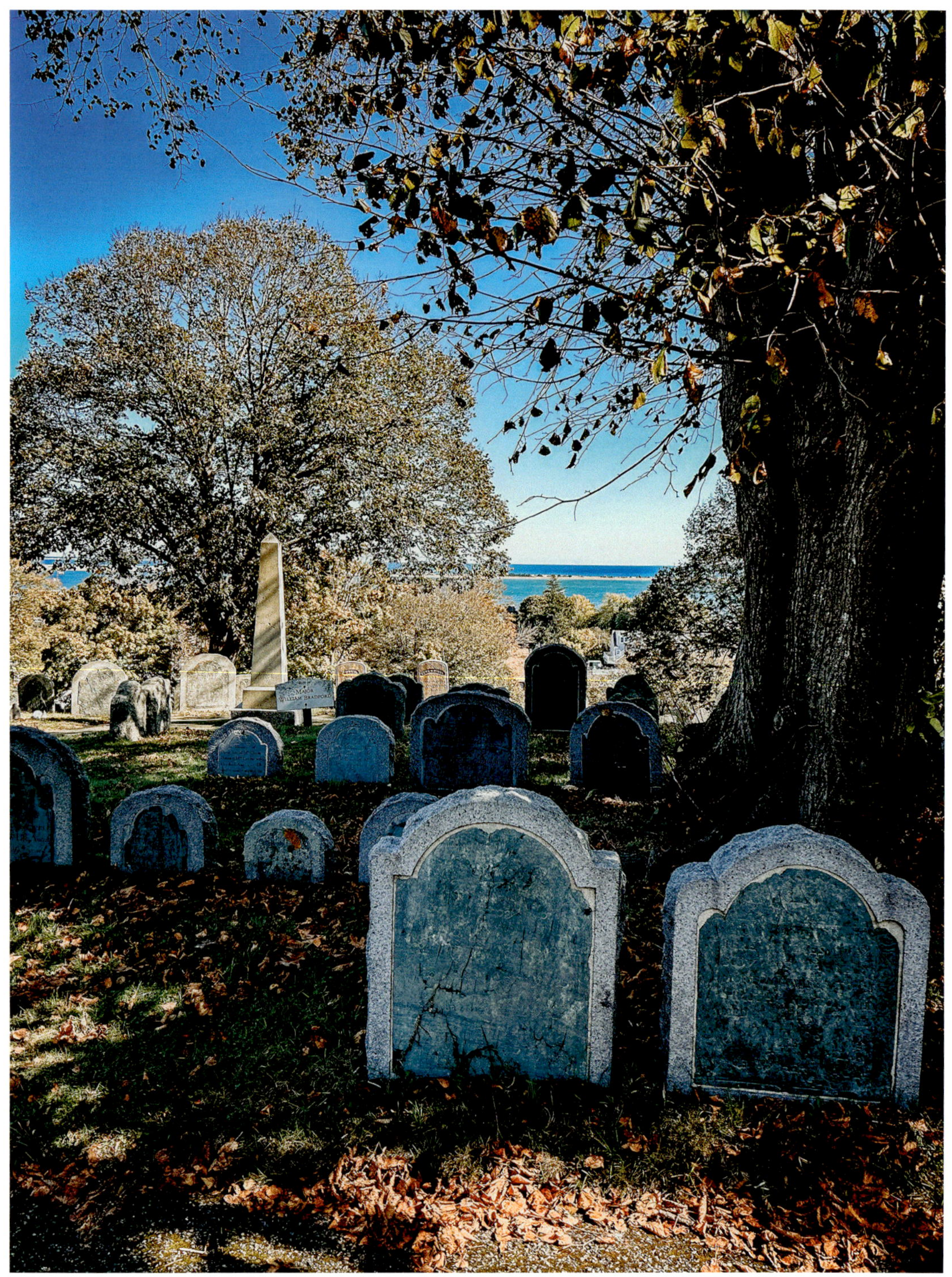

Many of the old markers are now encased in an extra layer of stone to help protect and preserve them.

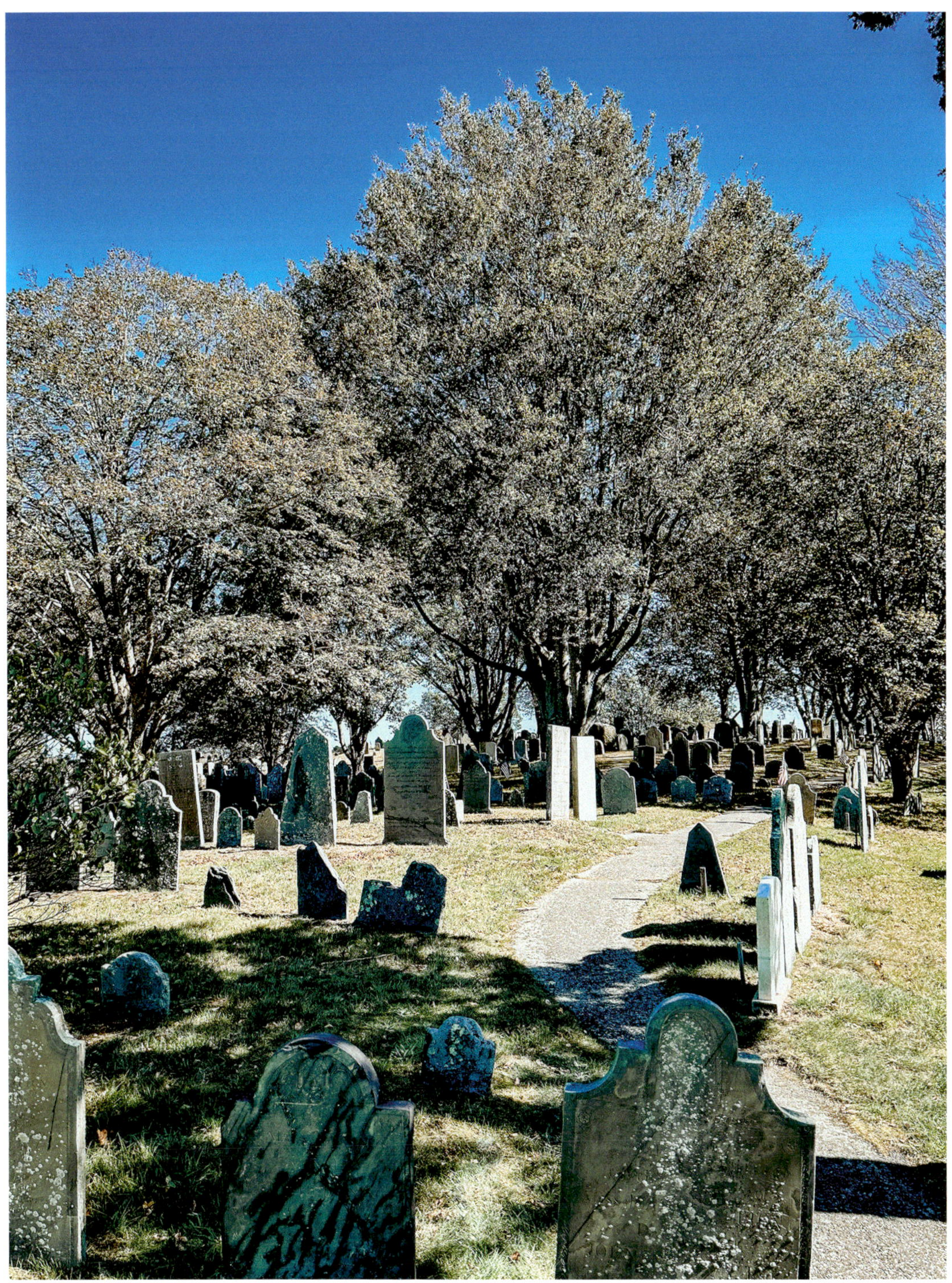

The winding paths and tight rows of tombstones leave Burial Hill in Plymouth feeling like a "classic" New England cemetery.

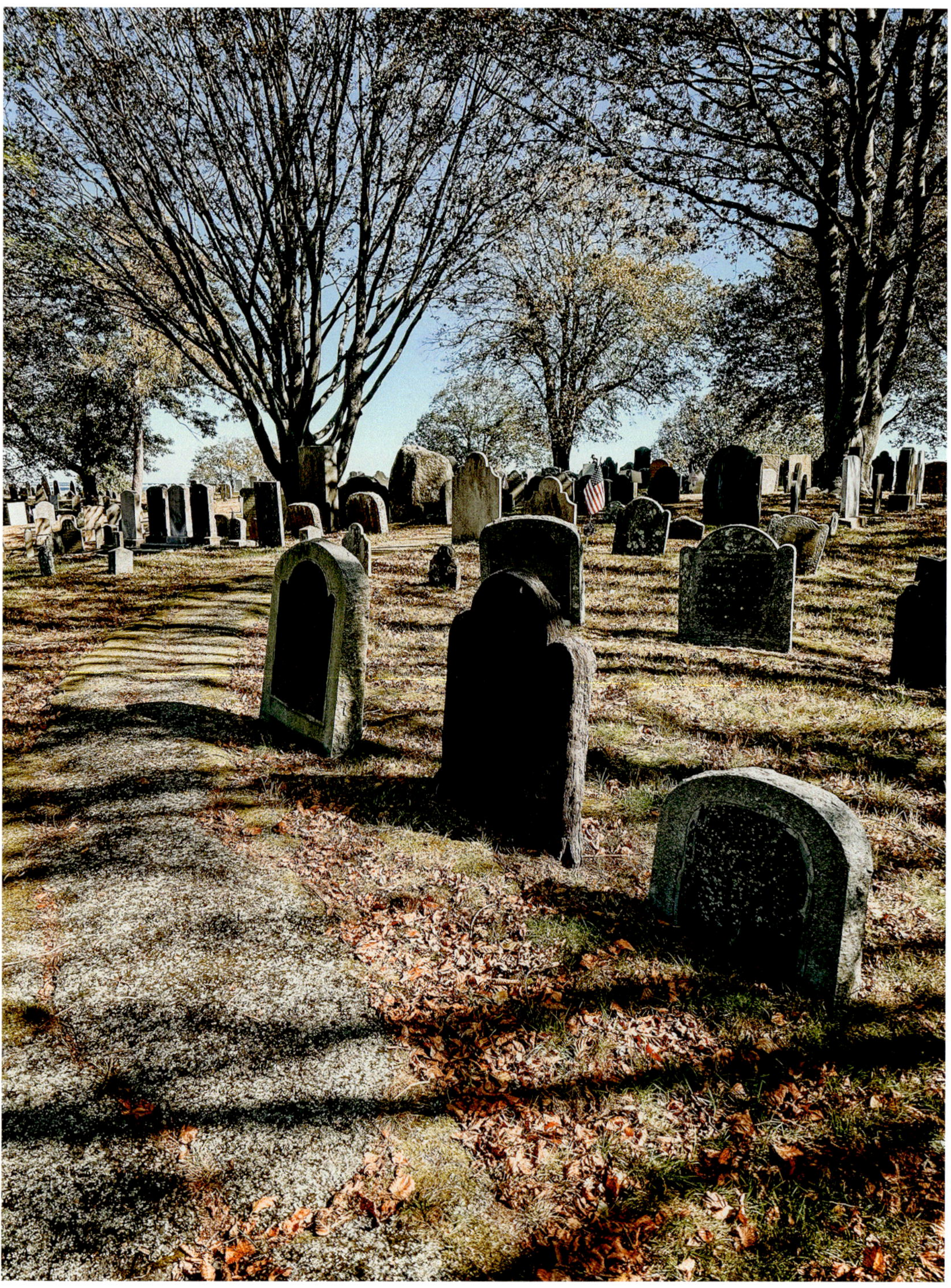

Fallen leaves add to the "classic" cemetery feel of this place in the autumn season.

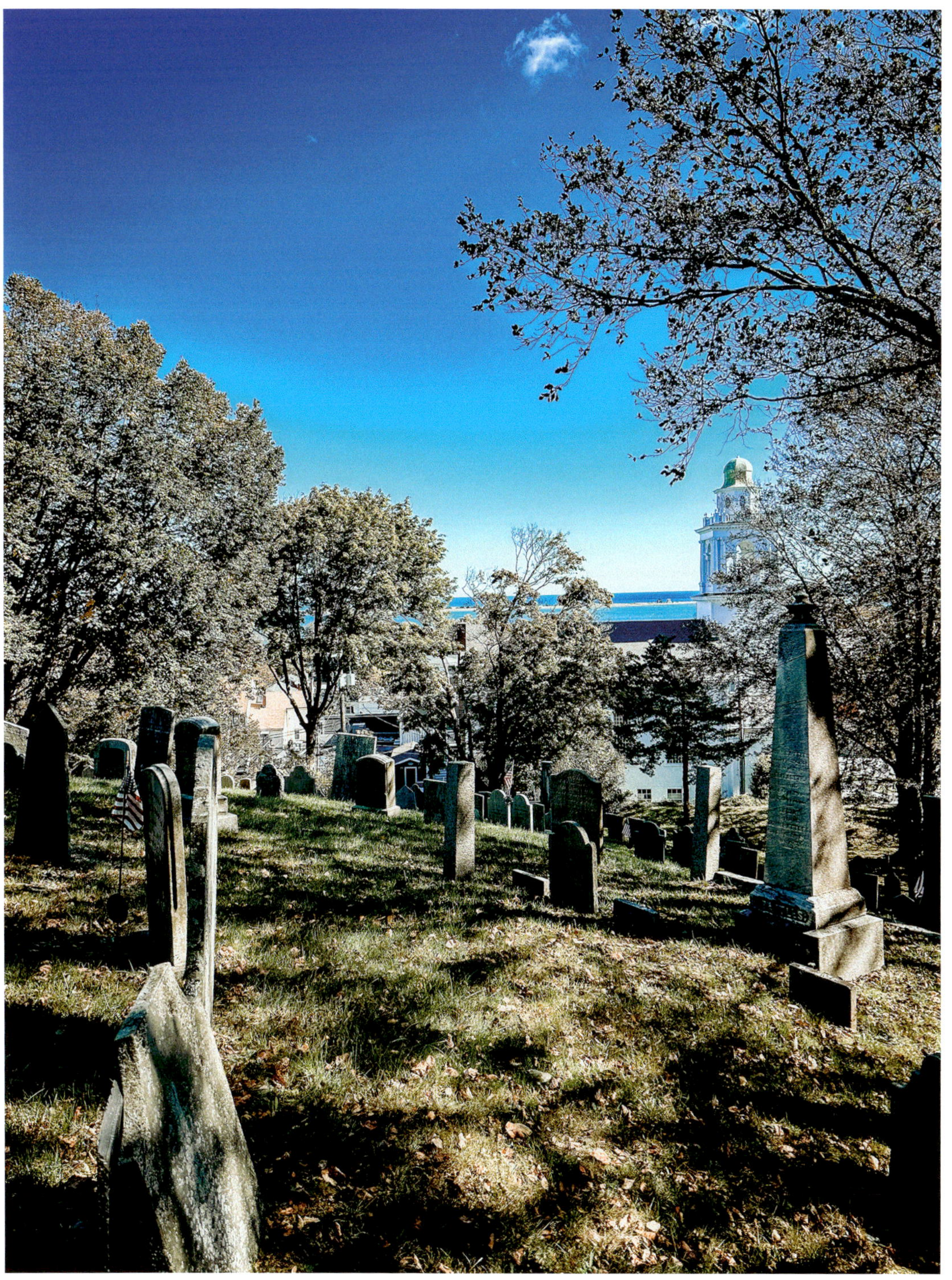

The view of the Church of Pilgrimage with the bay in the distance is one of my favorite views from Burial Hill.

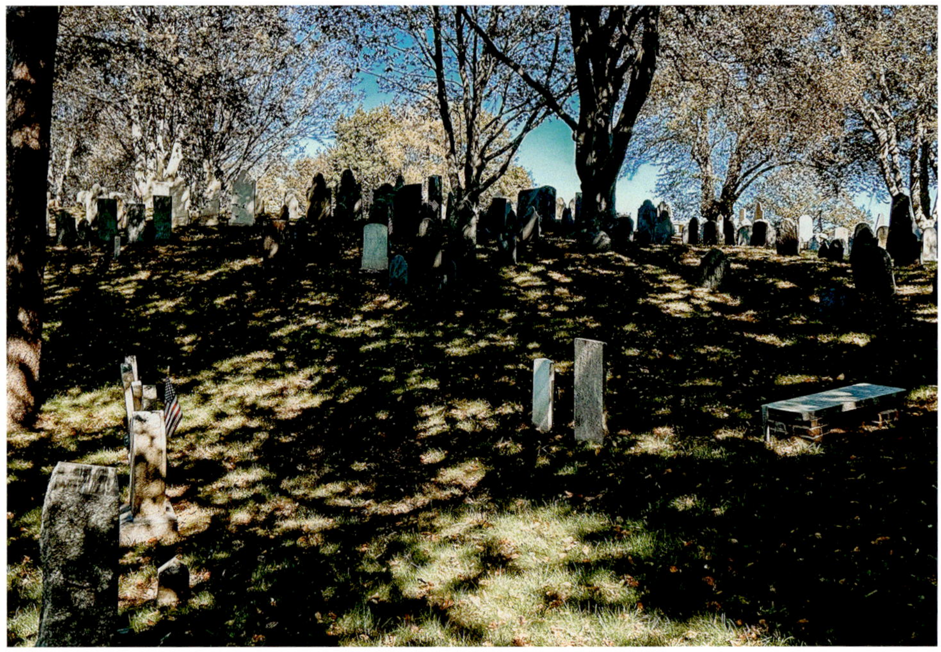

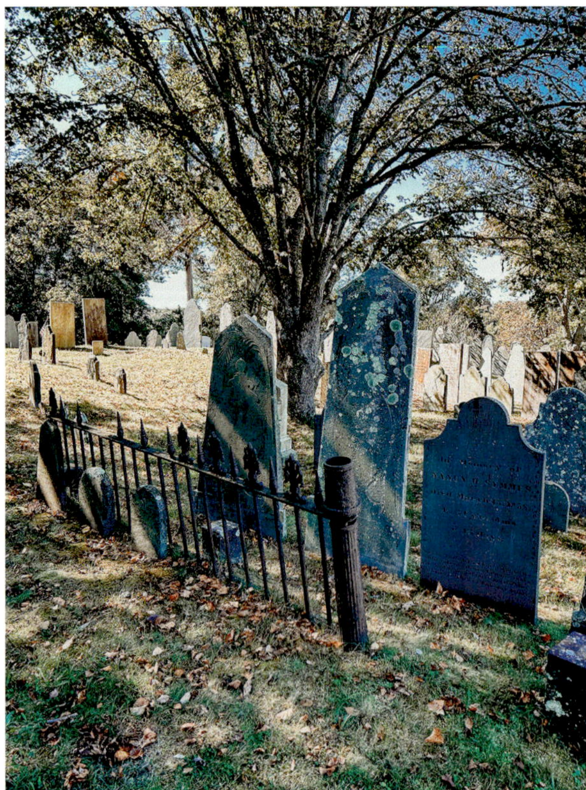

Above: Looking up the hill, you can get an idea of how many graves are at the top.

Left: What remains of a fence near these graves shows the cemetery's age.

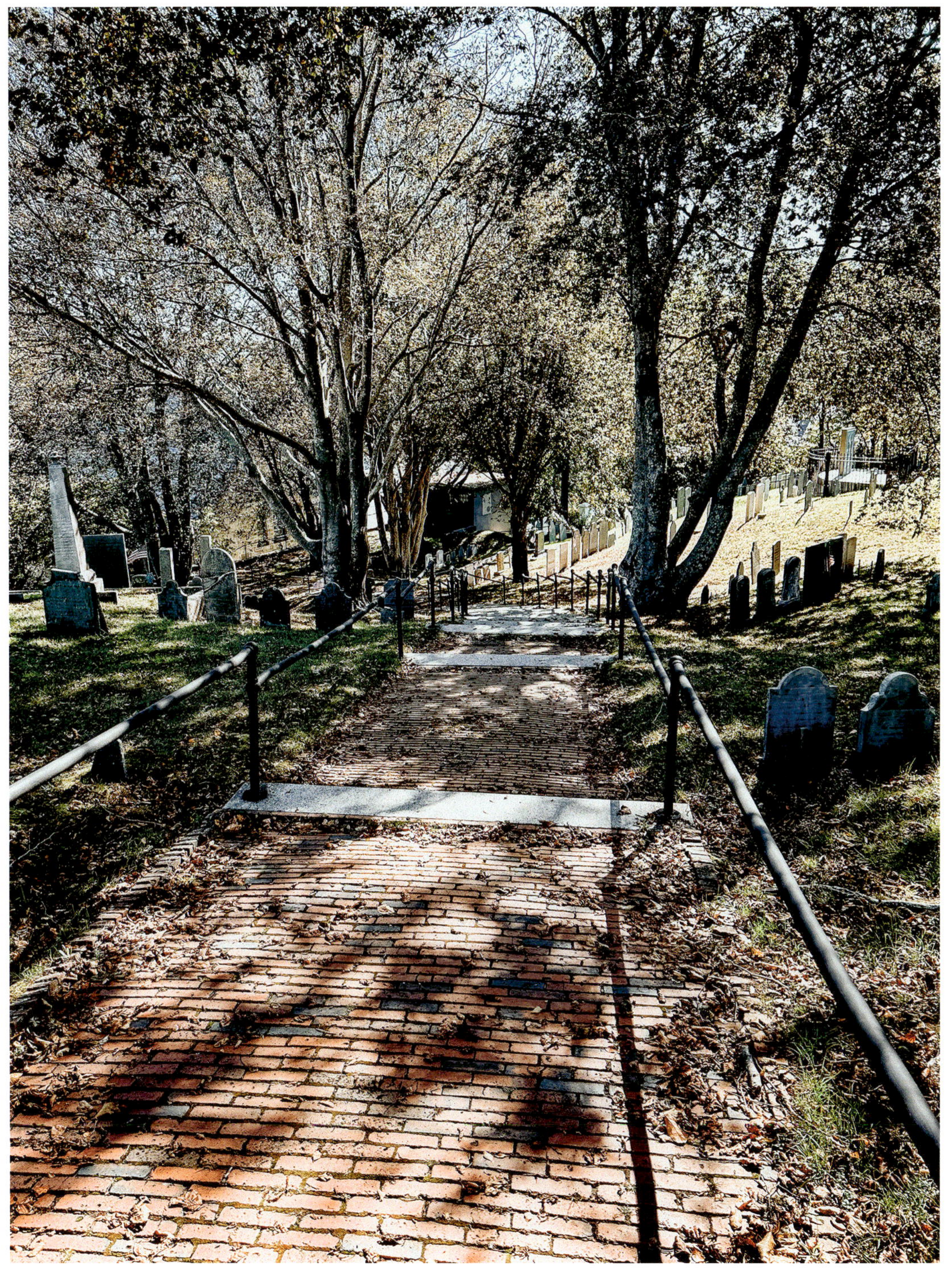

While the paths are narrow, the stairs are a bit wider and aren't as narrow as some older staircases can be. It can still feel like quite the walk to the top!

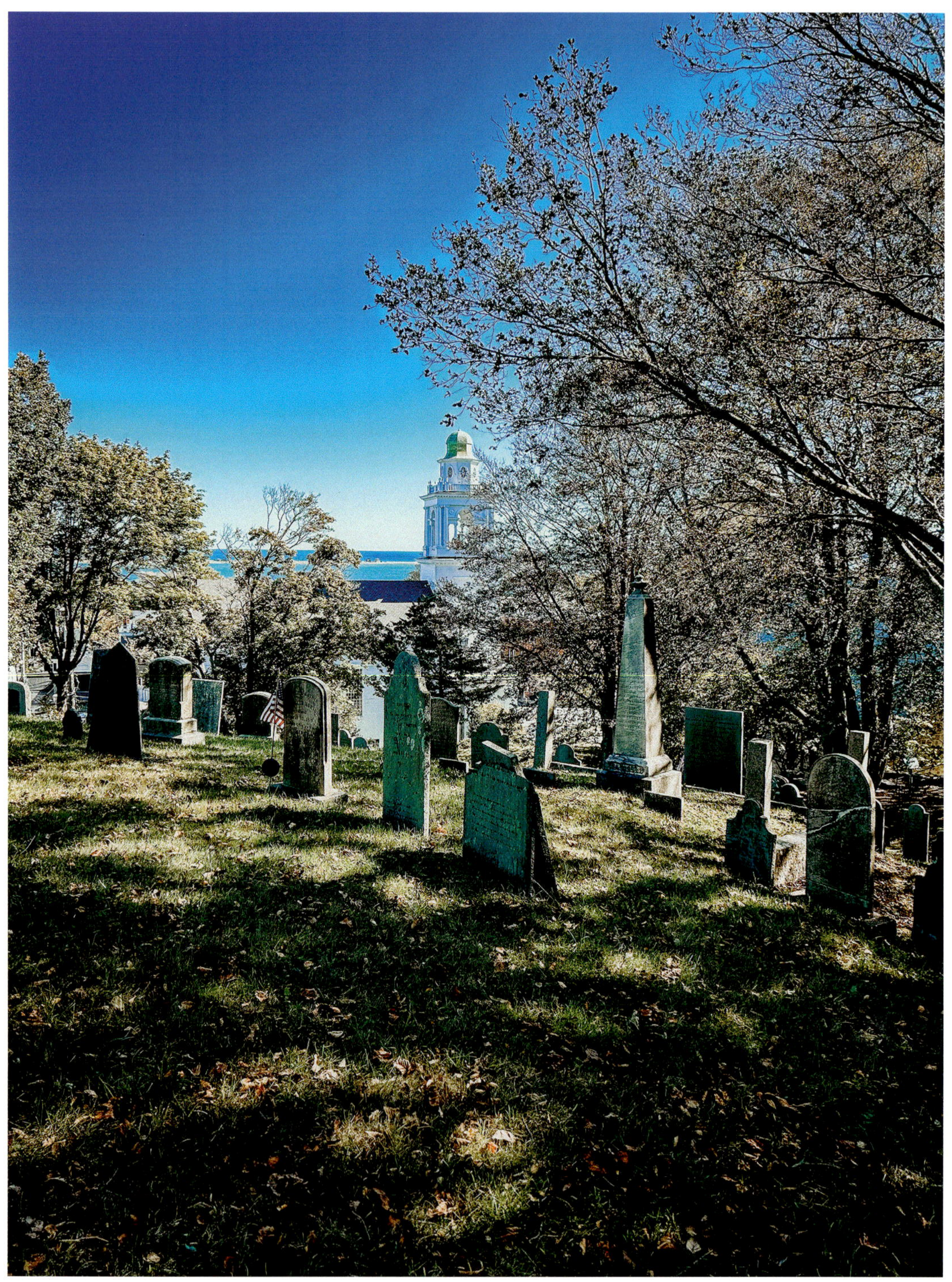

In this photo, you can see a few cracked and broken graves. Thankfully, many have been repaired and preserved through great efforts.

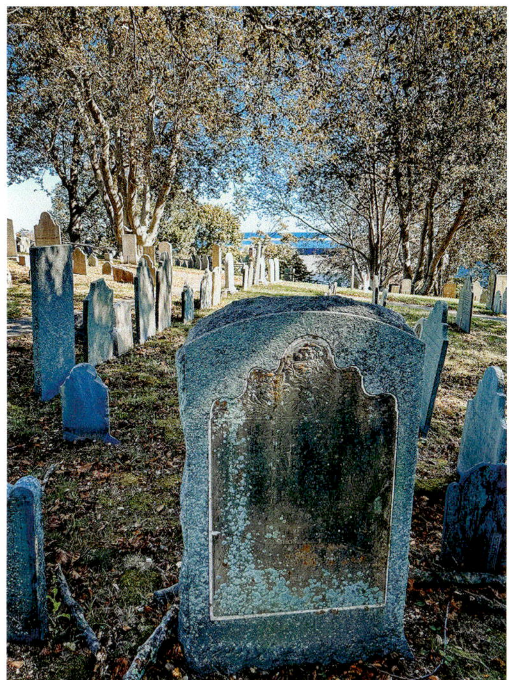

Right: While the stone grave markers are still standing, some of them are becoming weathered to time as well.

Below: In addition to being surrounded by history, the views of the bay from Burial Hill are unmatched.

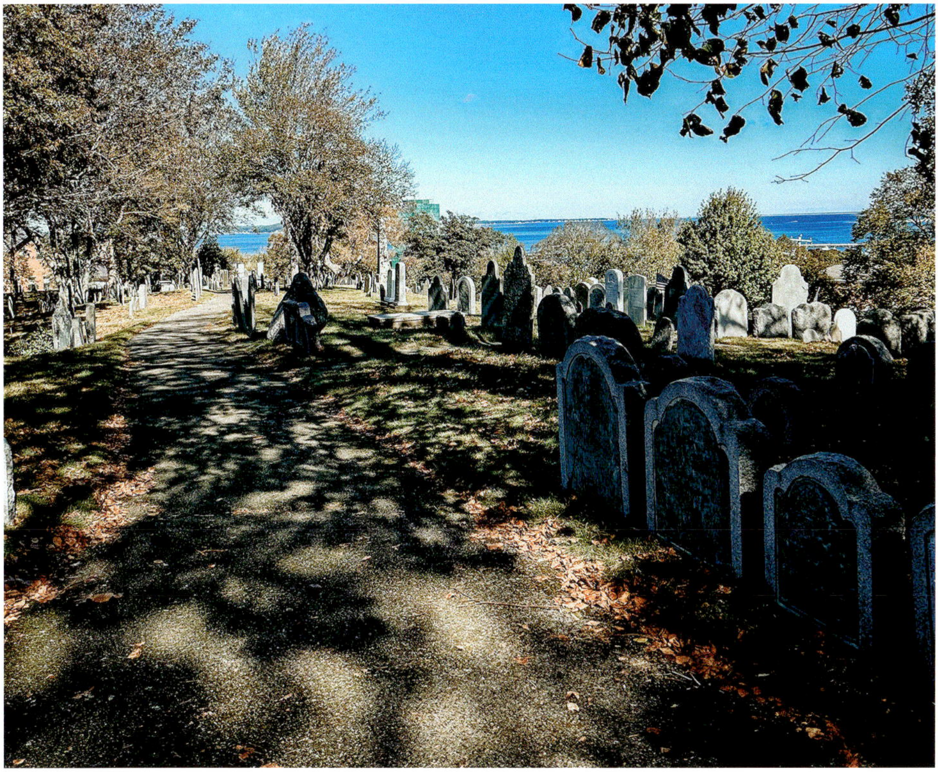

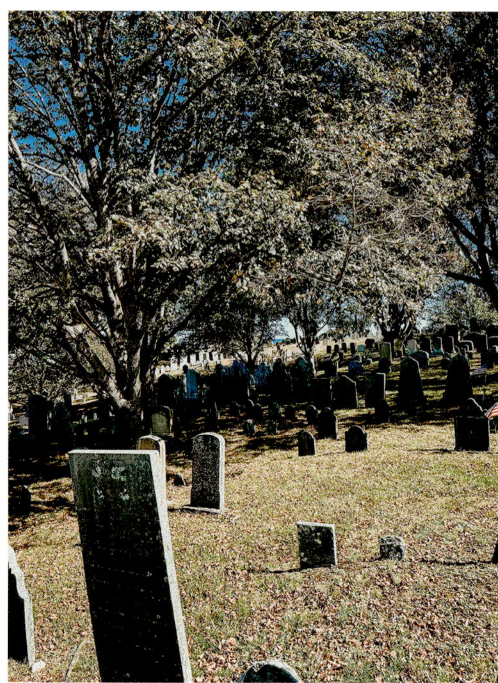

Left: The number of headstones seems never ending as you travel along the hill.

Below: Some of my favorite photographs were taken as I was walking up the hill.

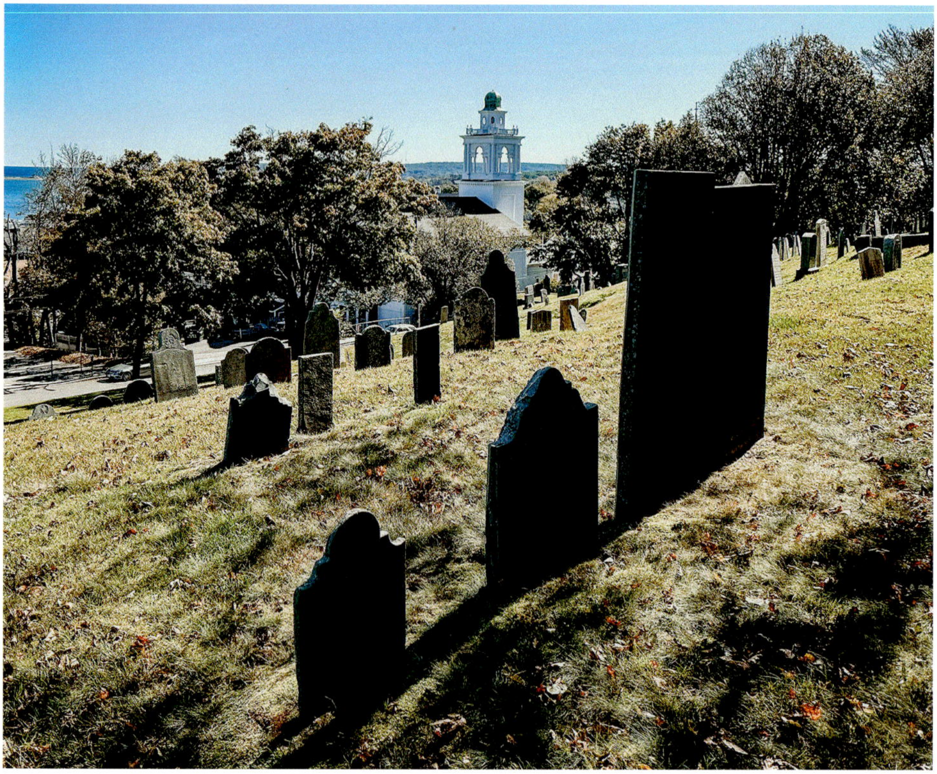

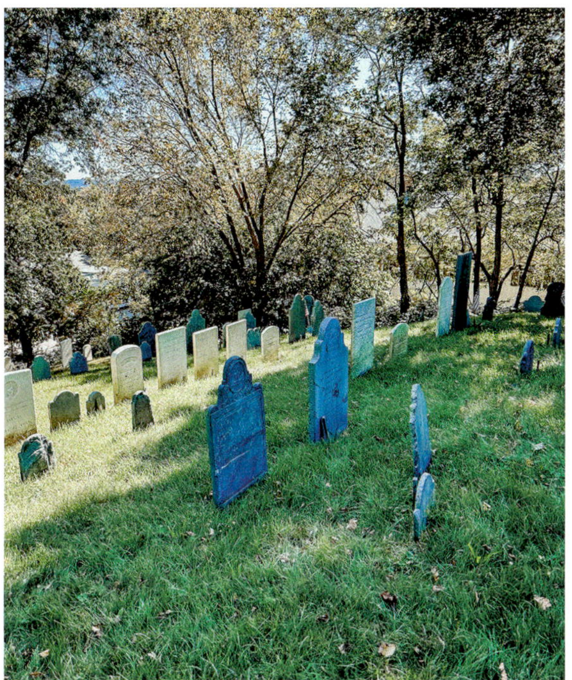

Of the approximately 2,200 headstones, 1,400 of them are made of sandstone, slate, or schist. Today, they're typically granite or marble.

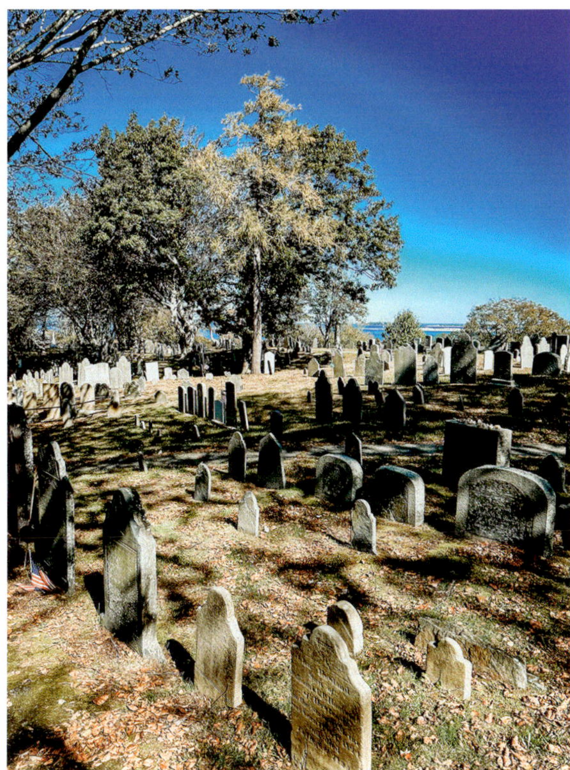

The last time I visited Burial Hill, I found myself alone as I walked the old paths between the graves, with nothing but time to photograph and take in the surrounding history in this peaceful spot.

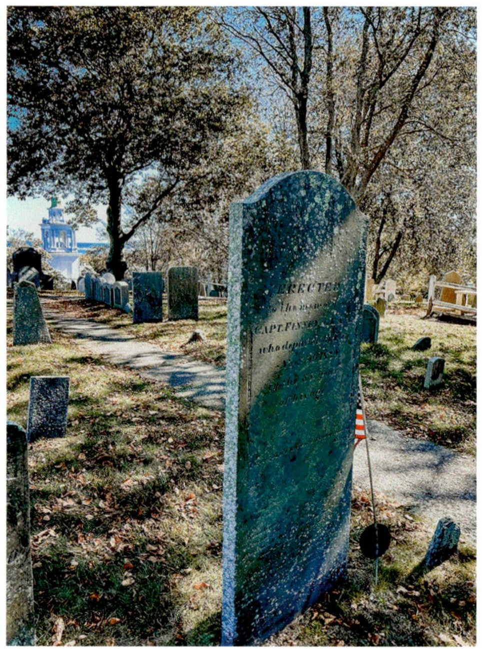

Left: The grave of Finney Leach, captain and father of nine, serves as a reminder: "Tread lightly o'er this sacred ground, a resting place for mortal man, free from all care which earth abounds, for this short life is but a span. Stop! view your bed of earthly clay and think how soon your race is run, prepare yourself without delay, for soon must be your setting sun."

Below: The hill is about 165 feet above sea level, overlooking the bay as well as the rest of Plymouth's historic downtown.

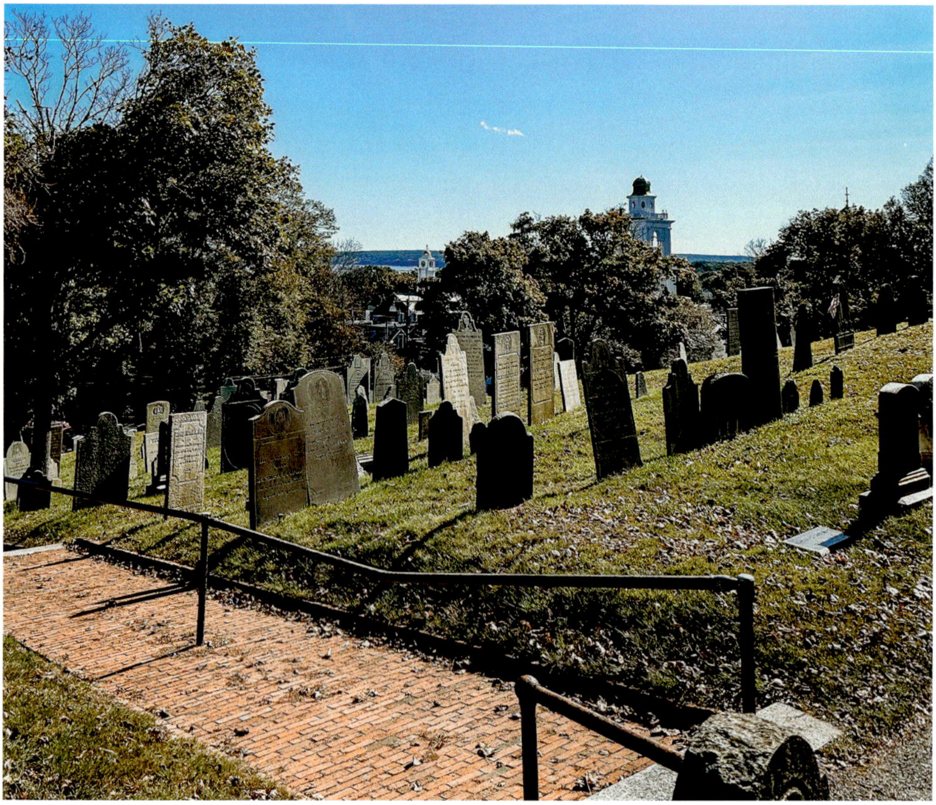

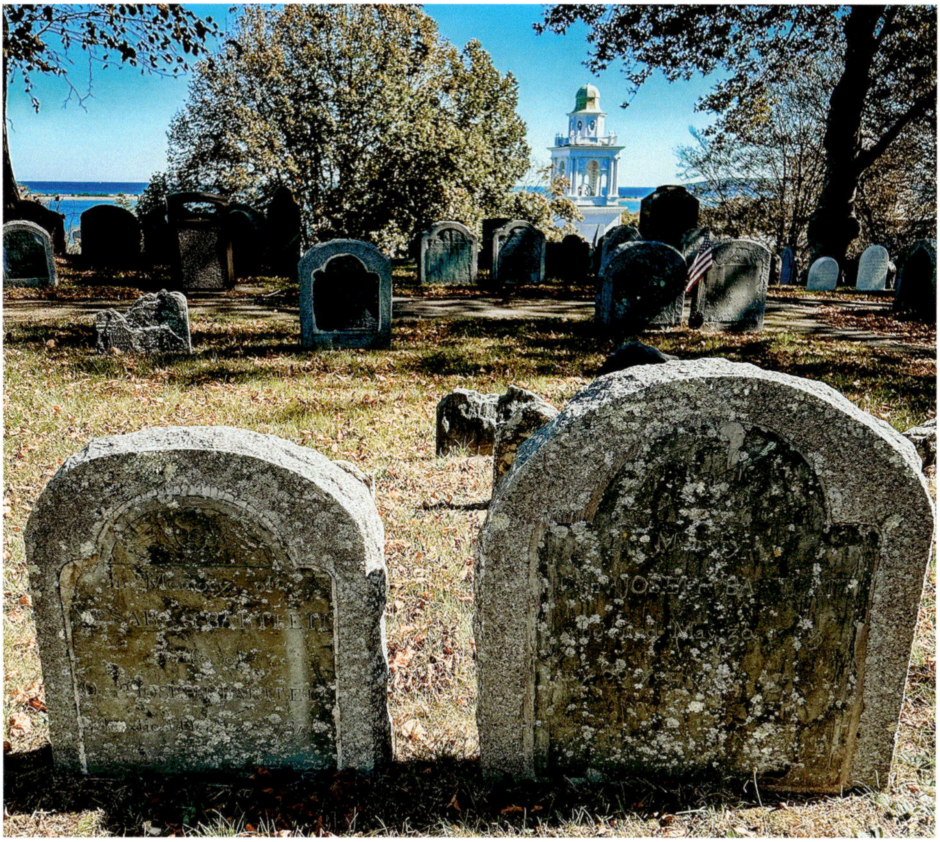

Above: These graves belong to Deacon Joseph and Mrs. Sarah Bartlett. They were married in 1727 and had six children together. Six is average (or even a little low compared to some of the numbers I've seen researching). For comparison, in 2023, the average number of children per household in the US was between one to two children

Right: When I am in an older cemetery, I can't help but wonder how long the trees have been there and how big they were when burials were first occurring.

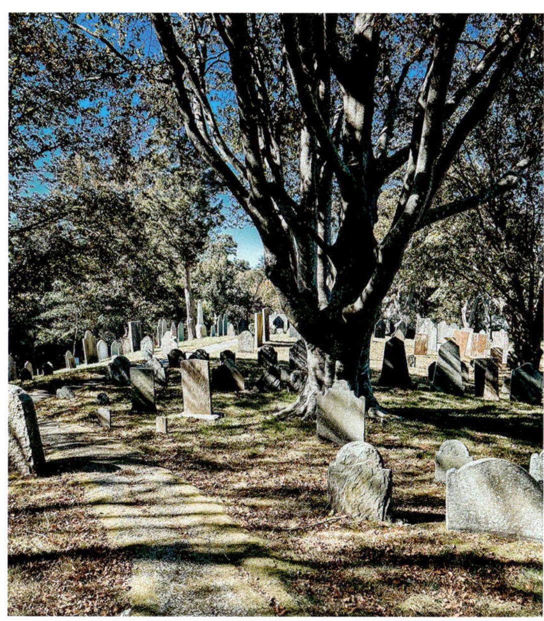

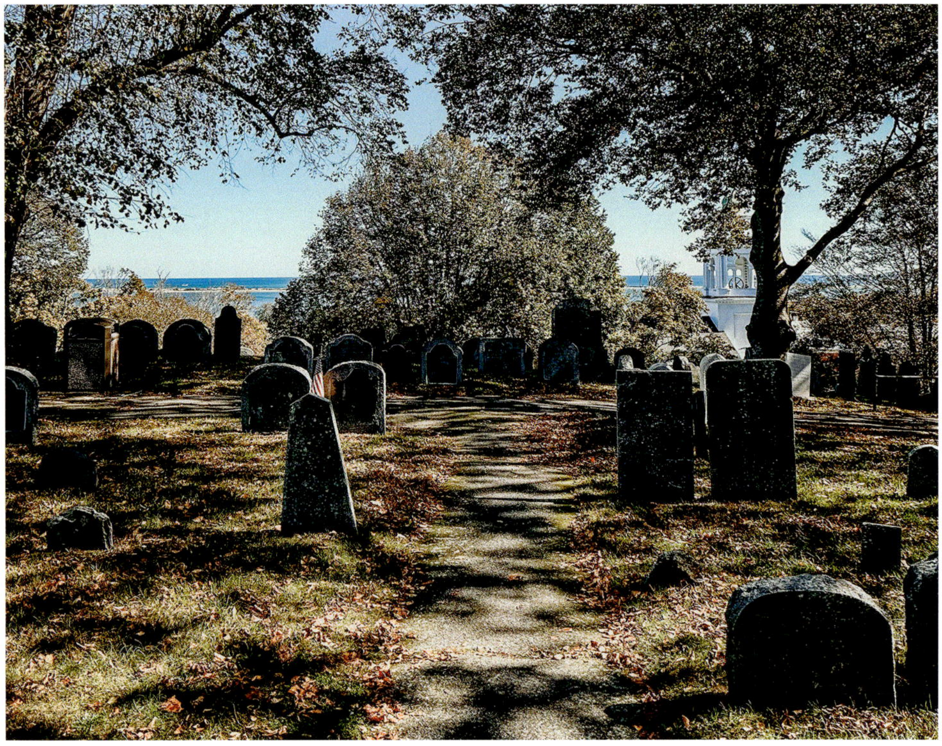

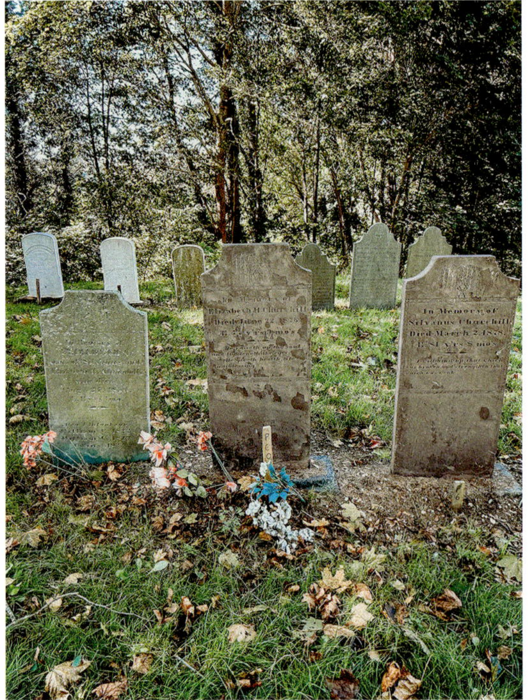

Above: When visiting Burial Hill, make sure to give yourself plenty of time to walk among the graves.

Left: Here are some of the Churchill family graves. The one in the center is Elizabeth; to her right is her husband Silvanus. While they both lived to old age, the grave to the left belongs to their daughter, Elizabeth, who died when she was eleven, as well as their infant sons (both named William).

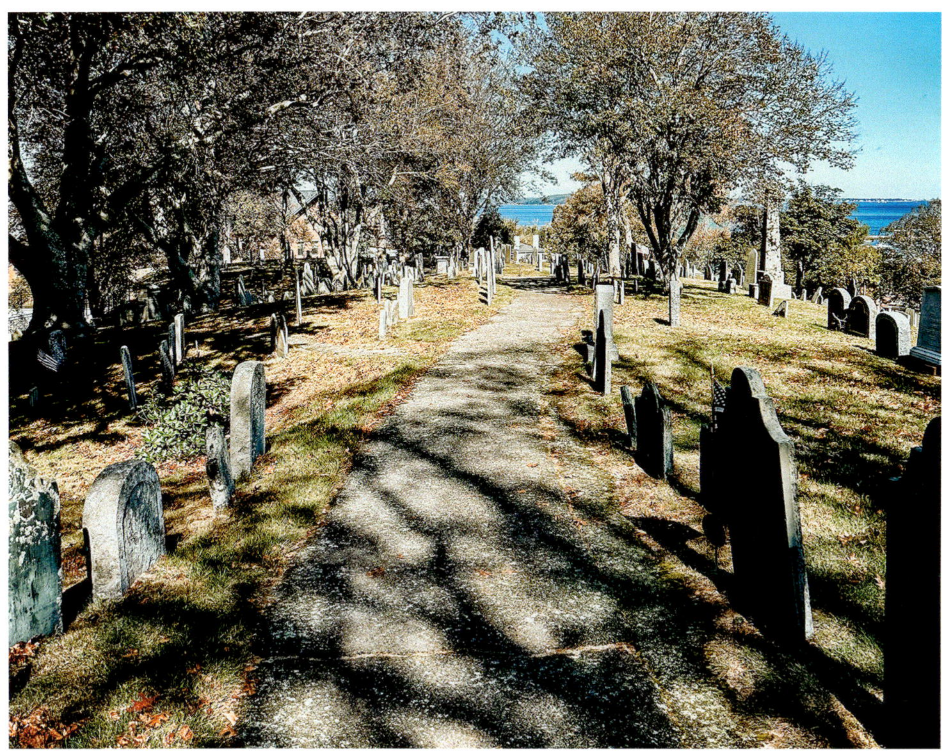

Above: Headstones line every narrow path within the cemetery.

Right: With many sea captains buried here as well as there being memorials to men lost at sea, it seems fitting that Burial Hill overlooks the bay.

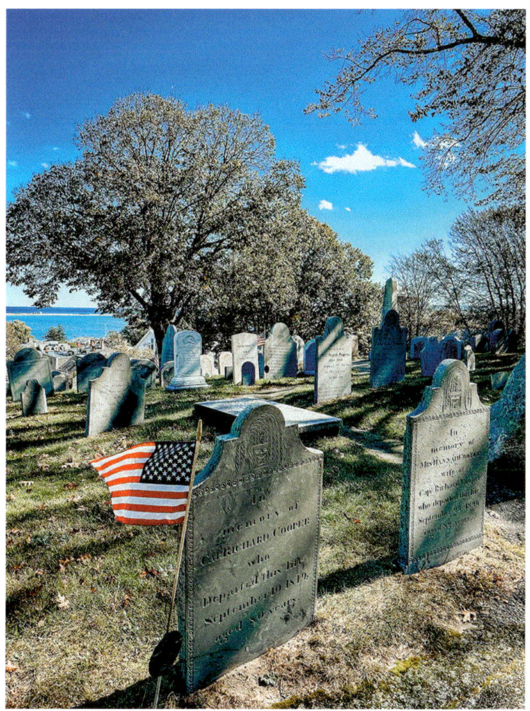

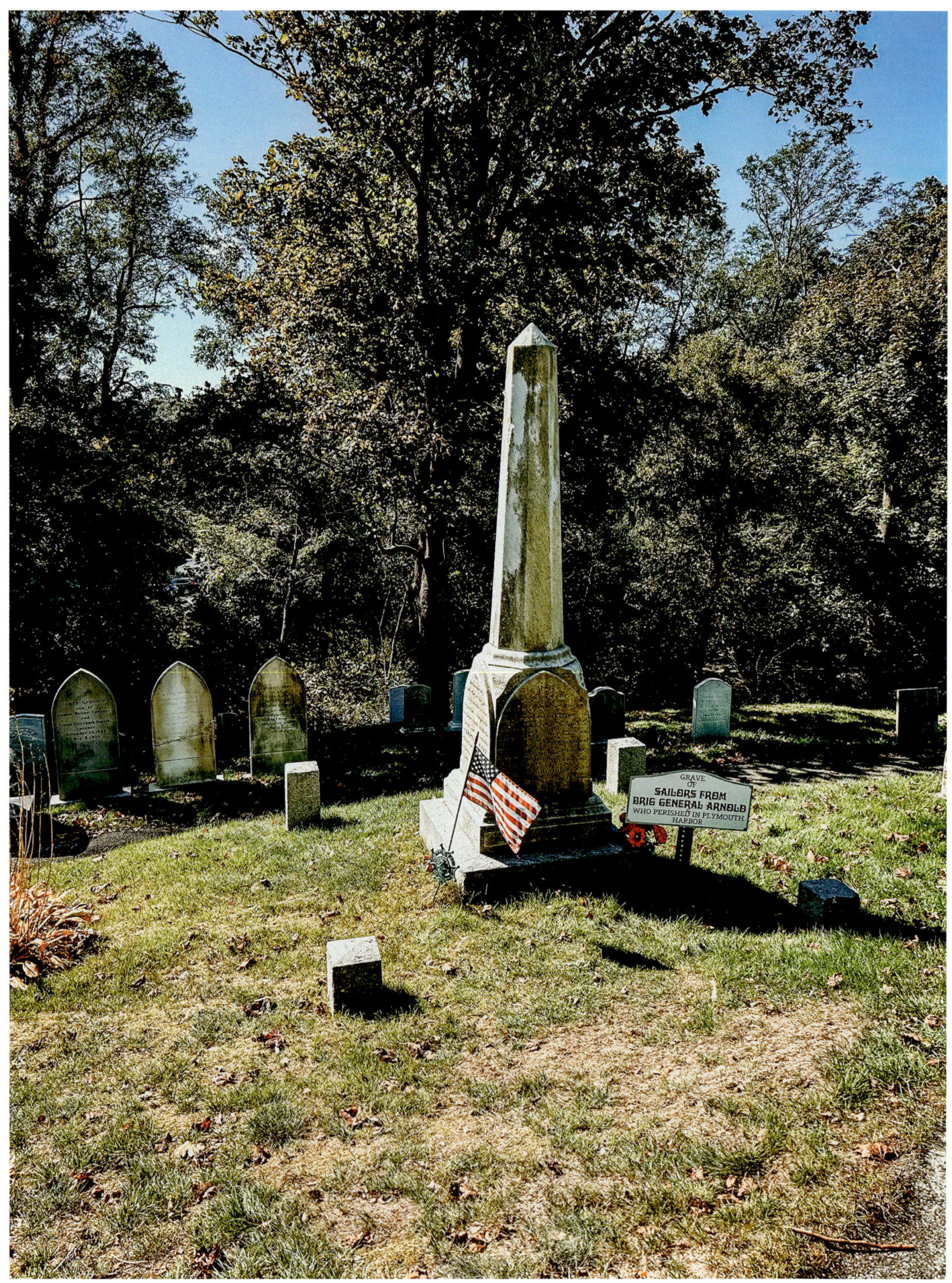

This obelisk marks the mass grave in the cemetery for the sailors lost in a shipwreck in 1778.

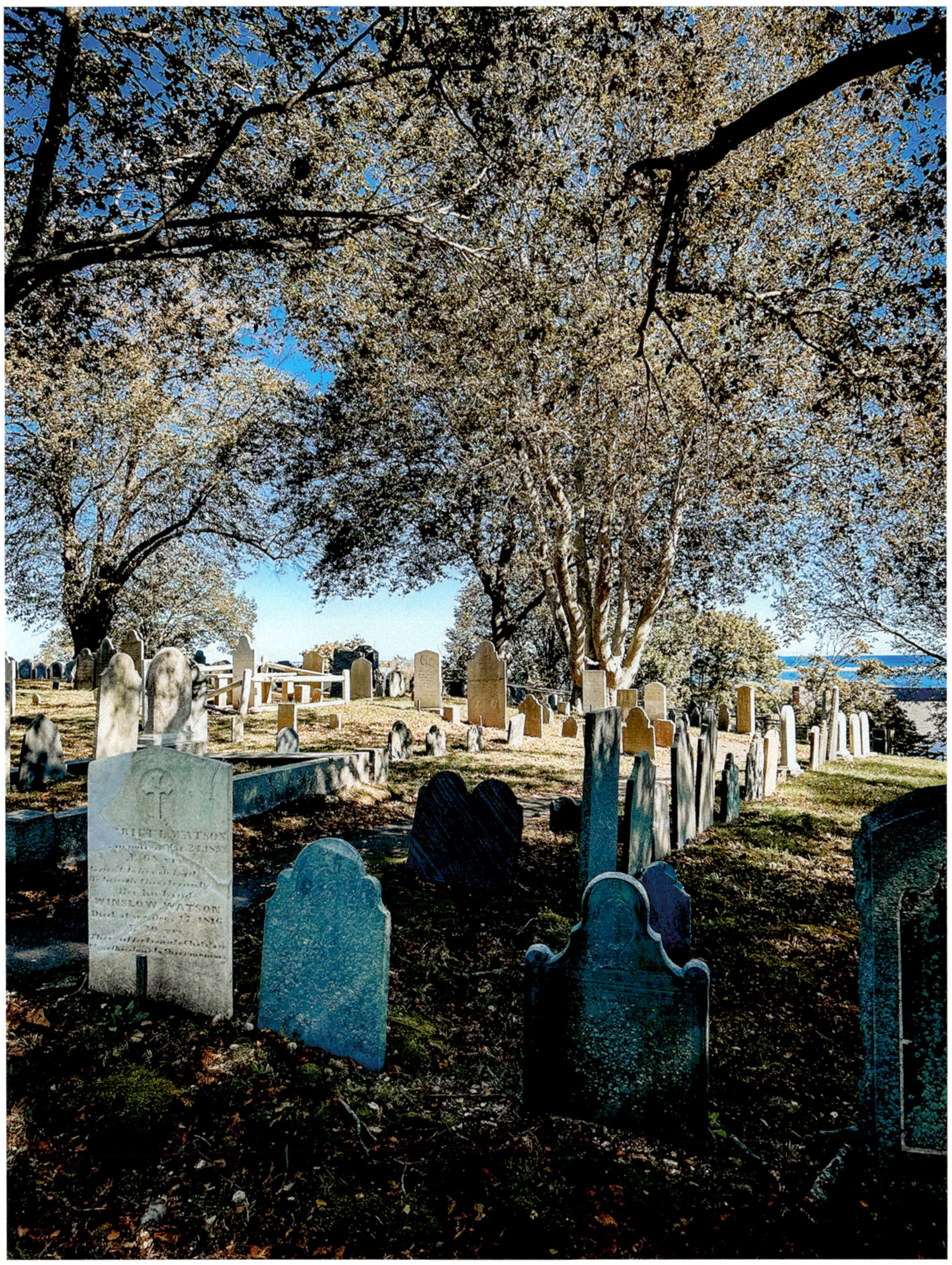

To the far left of this photo is the grave of Winslow Watson and his wife, Harriett. While Harriett lived to be sixty-eight, Winslow was lost at sea when he was only thirty. "Their affectionate children place this stone to their memory."

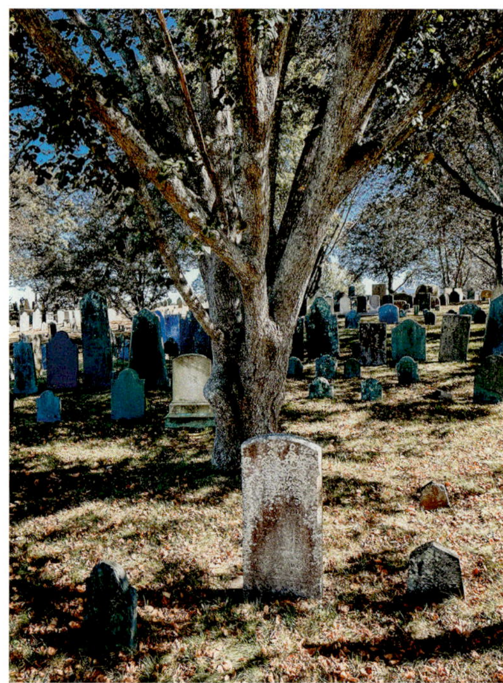

Left: Each grave has an opportunity to tell a unique story.

Below: Near the grave of John Howland from the *Mayflower* is an almost completely illegible stone due to weathering as well as lichen growth. The graves of this cemetery truly come in all shapes, sizes, and conditions.

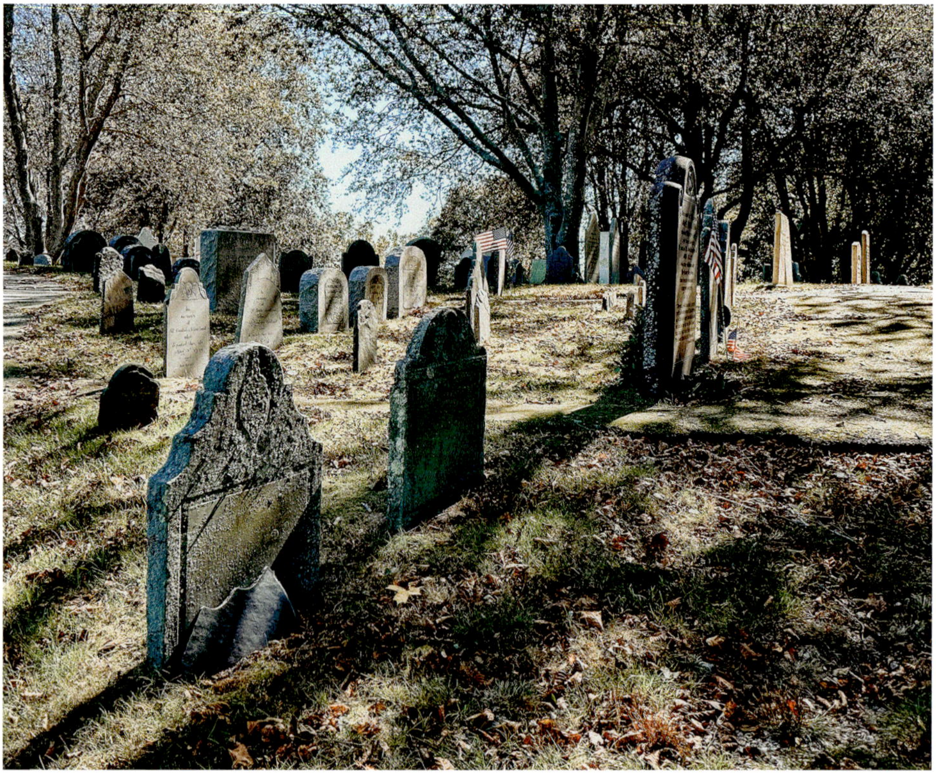

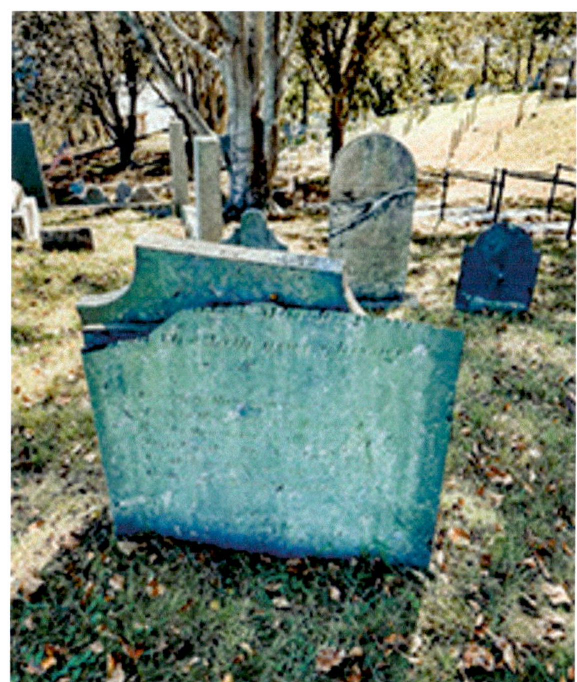

This grave shows how fragile the stones are in older cemeteries; it's broken to where I can't tell you who is buried here. Please take care while visiting.

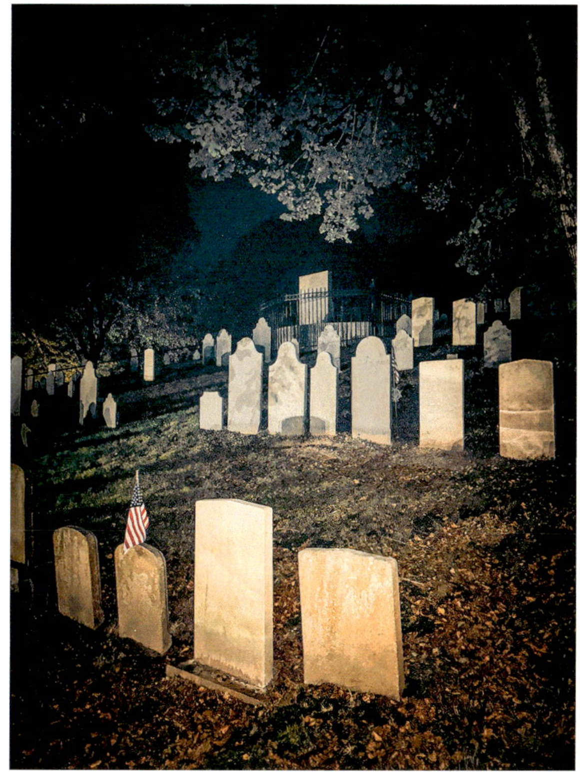

There will be a few night photos of the cemetery throughout this book. They were taken while on a history/ghost tour that had permission to visit the cemetery at night. Please follow all the rules and regulations when visiting these historical sites.

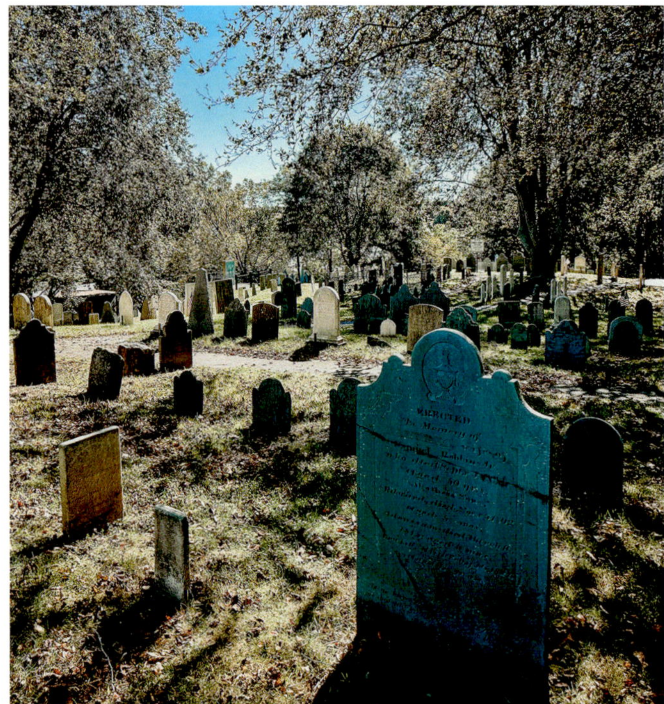

There are thousands of graves lining this hill.

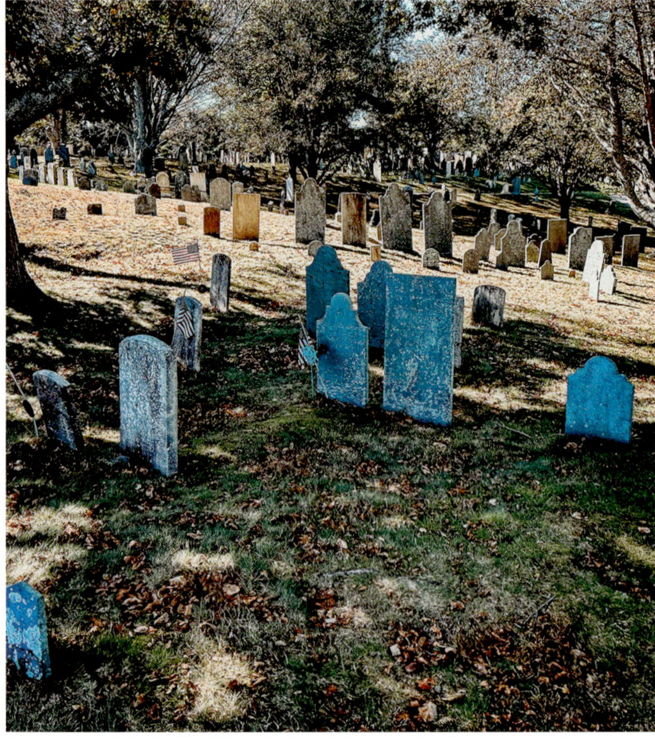

The cemetery is about five acres in all. With 2,269 headstones, that's about 453 headstones per acre.

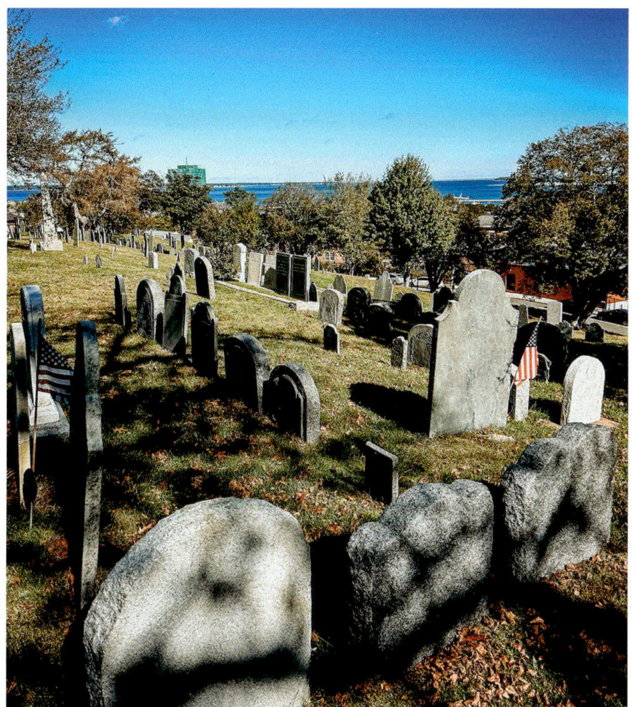

Many of the American flags and other markers to denote veterans were placed in the cemetery in 1914, which would have been around the time of WWI.

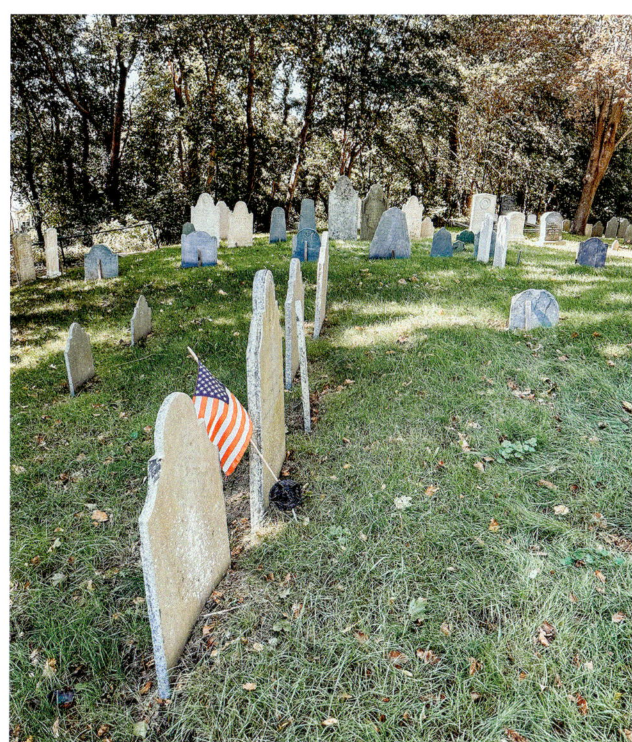

More American flags are dotted throughout the cemetery. With most burials taking place in 1850 or earlier, these veterans would most likely be from the Revolution or the War of 1812.

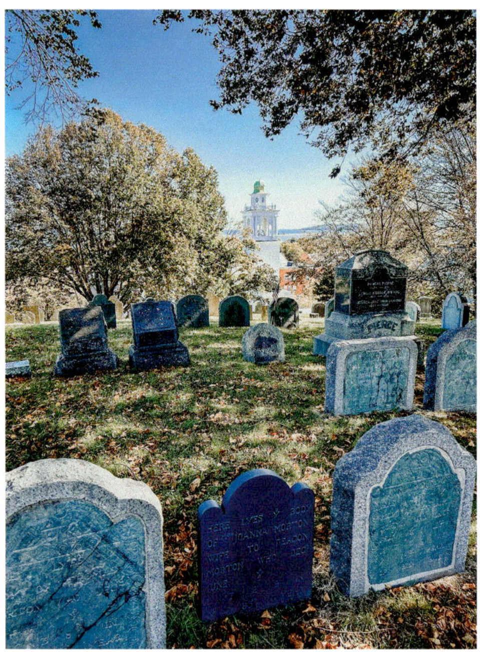

Left: The majority of the headstones at Burial Hill are from 1850 or earlier; most of the older graves are at the top of the hill.

Below: Here are some of the Morton family graves. These "newer" graves are further from the top of the hill as they are from the mid to late 1800s.

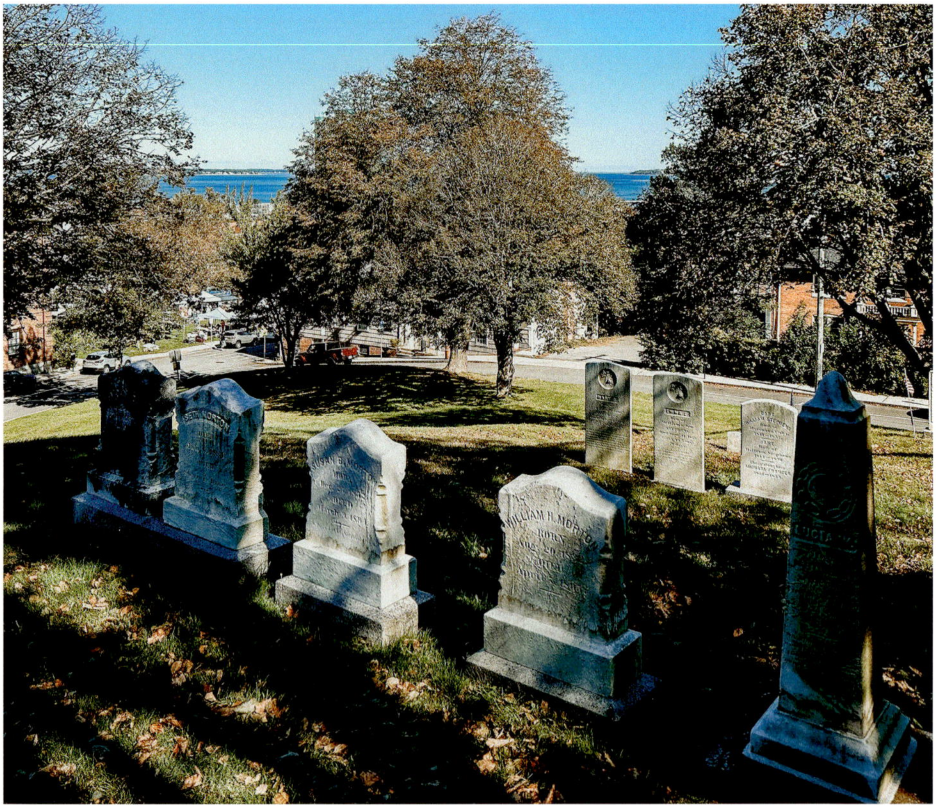

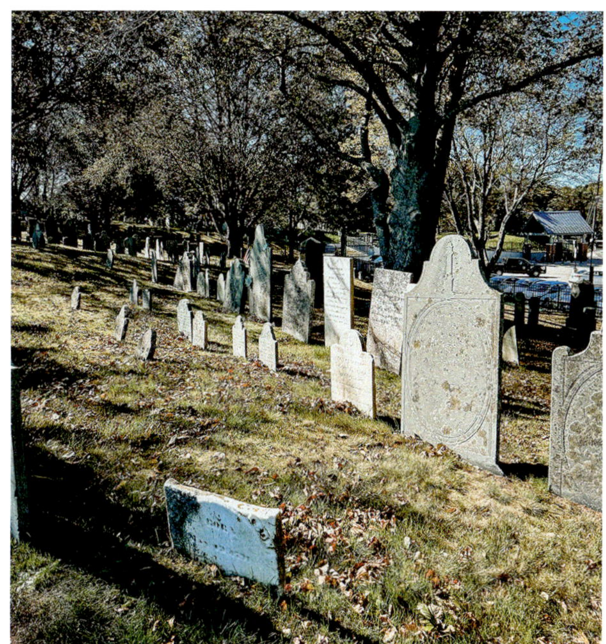

Sadly, not every grave can be saved/preserved. Some are broken beyond repair while others have begun to sink further into the ground.

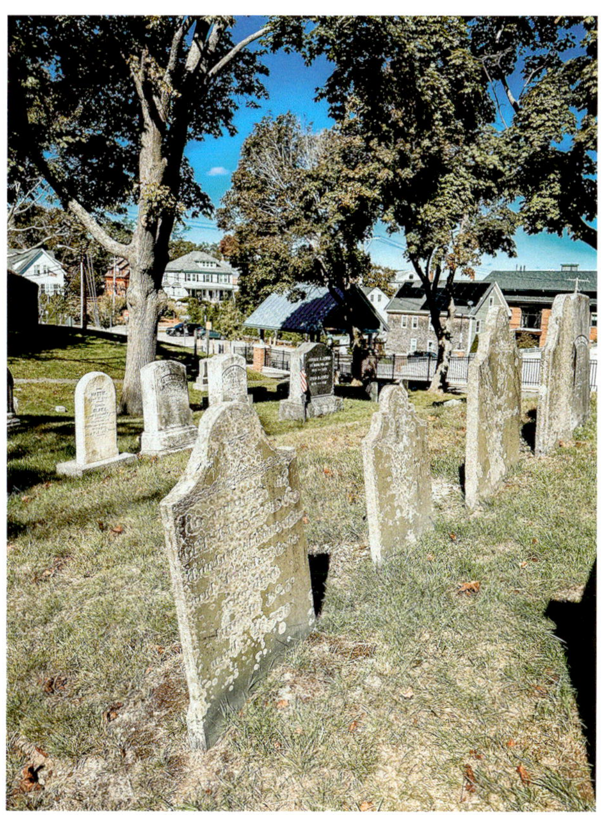

Some of the graves are getting harder to read as lichen is growing on them; this is very common, especially in older cemeteries.

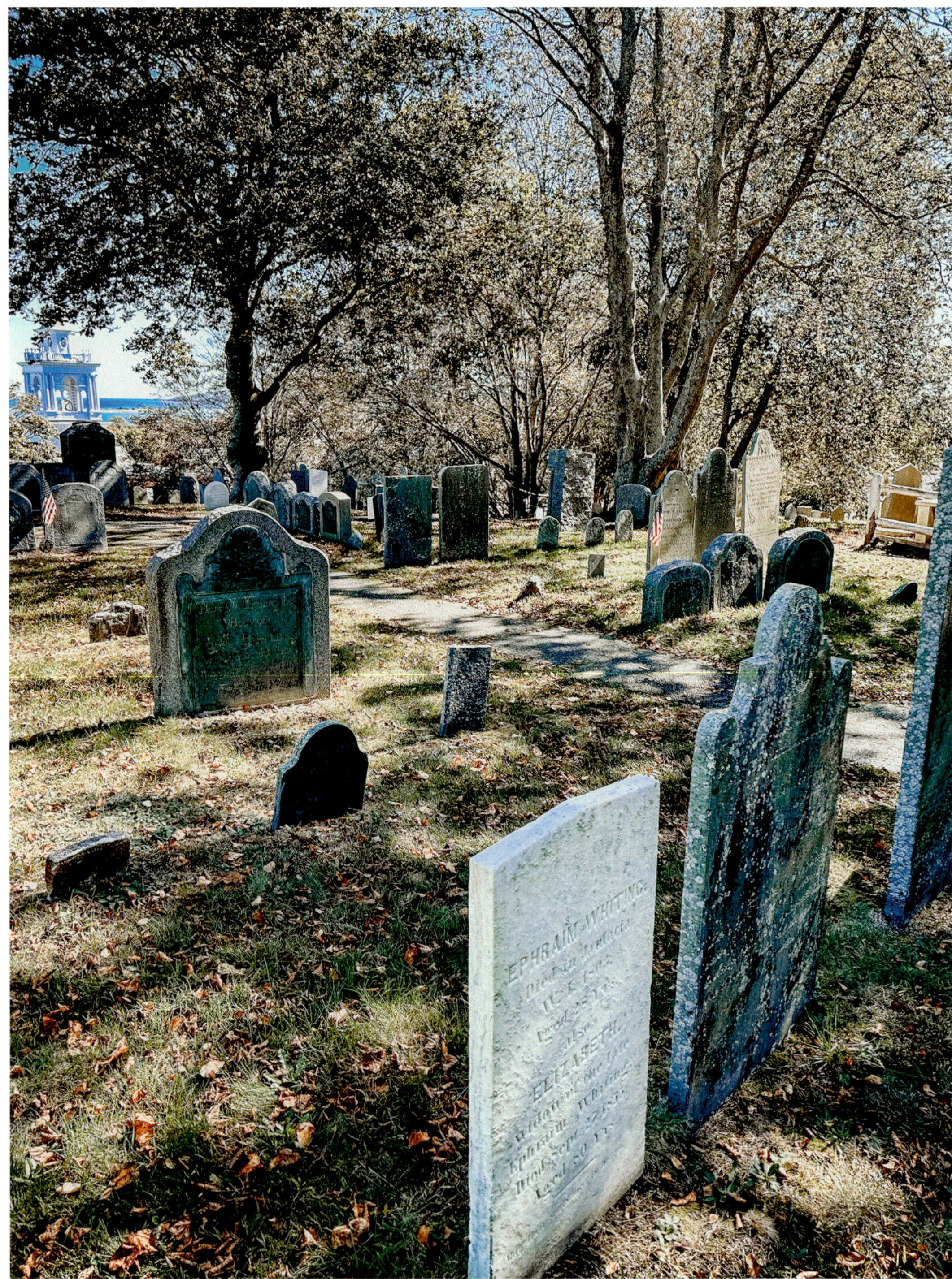

There are more stories in this cemetery than I would be able to fit into this book.

2

ℋISTORICAL GRAVES:
NOTABLE NAMES

The first governor of Plymouth Colony, William Bradford, is buried in this cemetery. Living from 1590–1657, he was no stranger to loss. His father died when he was only a year old; he went to live with his grandfather when his mother remarried. He lost his grandfather when he was six and his mother when he was seven.

He married Dorothy May in 1613, and they had their only son, John, in 1618. Of course, in 1620, he would sail to America aboard the *Mayflower*. The Pilgrims originally intended to sail for Virginia but ended up on Cape Cod due to the winter weather. He left the ship to go find a place for them to settle. Shockingly, when he returned, he found out Dorothy had fallen overboard and drowned. He was now a single father to a two-year-old in a foreign land.

He became governor in April of 1621 and held that position until his death in 1657, though with "five years exception" as noted on his grave. He remarried Alice Southworth in 1623. Along with a new wife he gained two stepchildren from her first marriage by which she was widowed: Constant and Thomas. William and Alice had three of their own children as well: William, Mercy, and Joseph.

Naturally, many recognize his name from the story of the first Thanksgiving, which was described in his journals.

On December 26, 1778, there was a horrific shipwreck just off the coast of Plymouth. The *General Arnold* shipwreck happened barely a mile offshore; they had left Boston on Christmas Eve and by Christmas Day realized there was a terrible storm and tried to shelter in Plymouth Bay. Wind pushed the ship towards shore (despite its anchor), and it eventually wrecked in the shallow water. Once there, it was battered by a combination of waves and wind from the storm. Despite being so close to the town, the townspeople were unable to help because of the waves. They couldn't get to the ship until the 28th, and by then seventy-two of the one hundred and five men, soaked from the waves and cold from the winter winds, had frozen to death. Sixty of those seventy are buried here in a mass grave. Their captain, James Magee, survived; he was buried with his men after his death twenty-three years later.

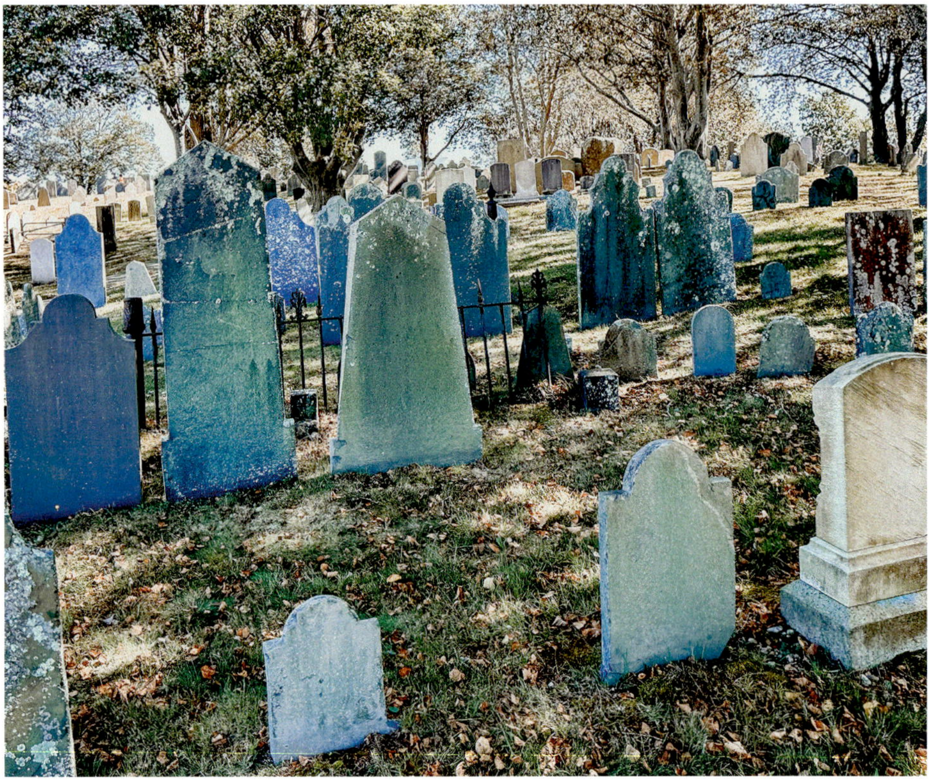

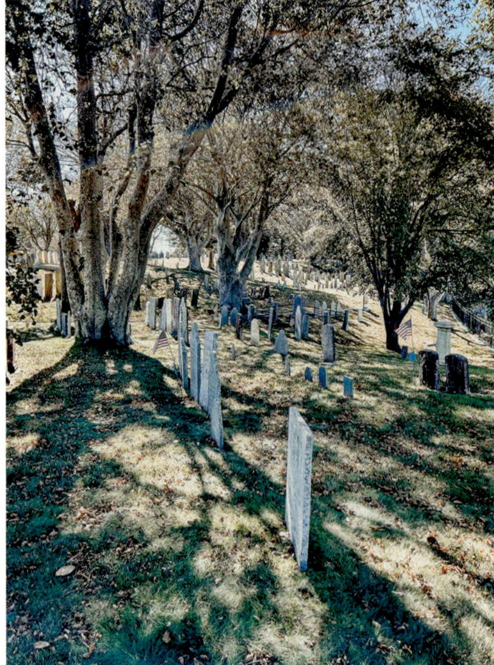

Above: The oldest known grave in the cemetery is from 1681, belonging to Edward Gray. While there may be older graves, they are unmarked as the grave marker was lost to time.

Left: It is easy to see how fragile some of these older stones are. Please take care while visiting here (or any other cemetery for that matter).

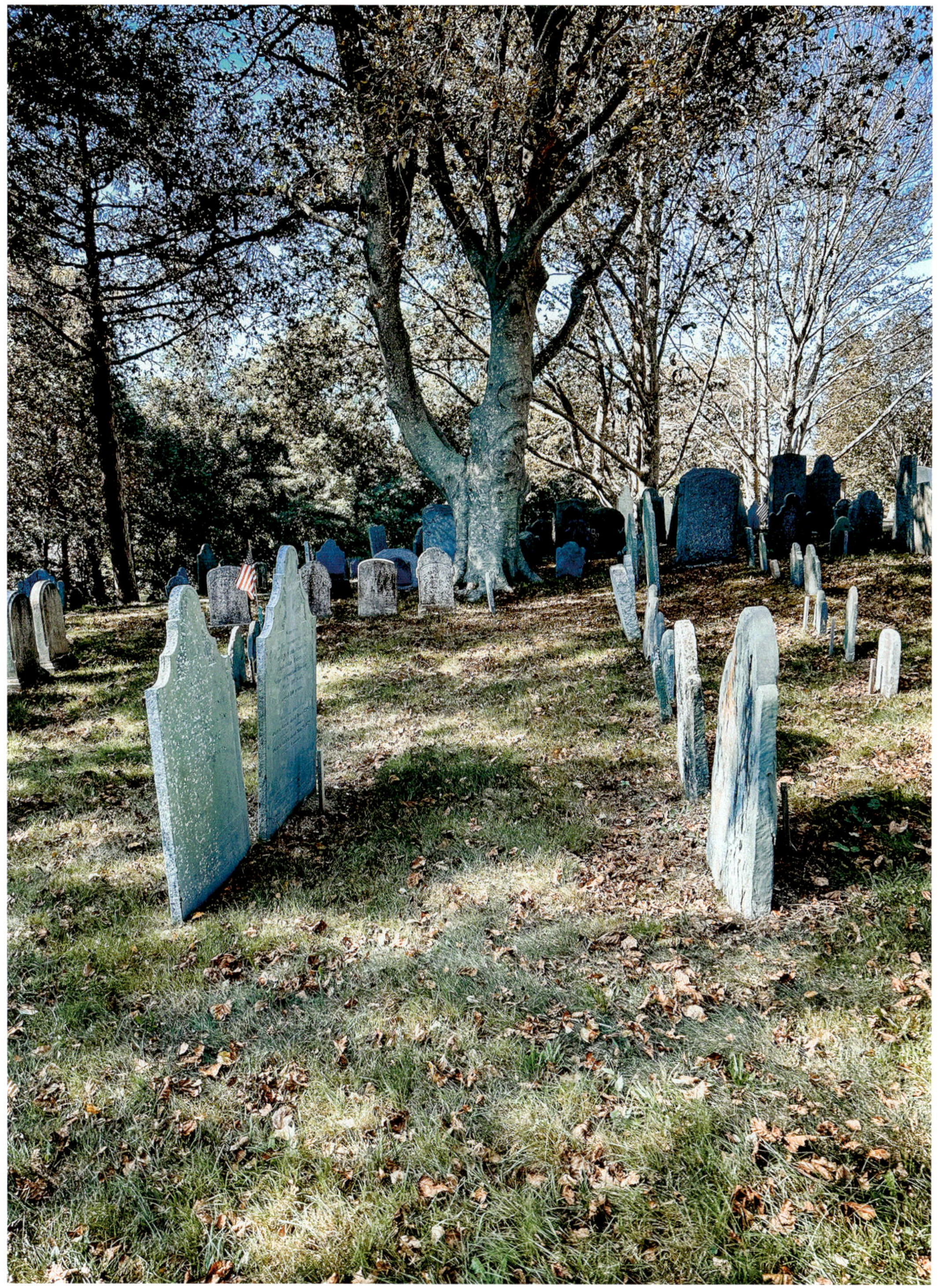

Many of the historical graves are shown to be so thin.

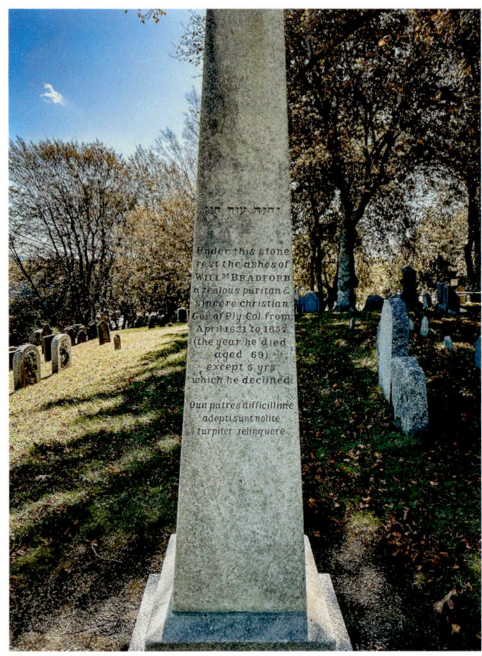

Left: "Under this stone rest the ashes of Willm. Bradford, a zealous puritan and sincere Christian. Gov. of Ply. Col. from April 1621 to 1657 (the year he died aged 69) except 5 years which he declined. *Quae patres difficillime adepti sunt nolite turpiter relinquere.*" (What the fathers with greatest difficulty effected do not basely abandon.)

Below: The obelisk marking the grave of William Bradford stands tall among the rest of the tombstones.

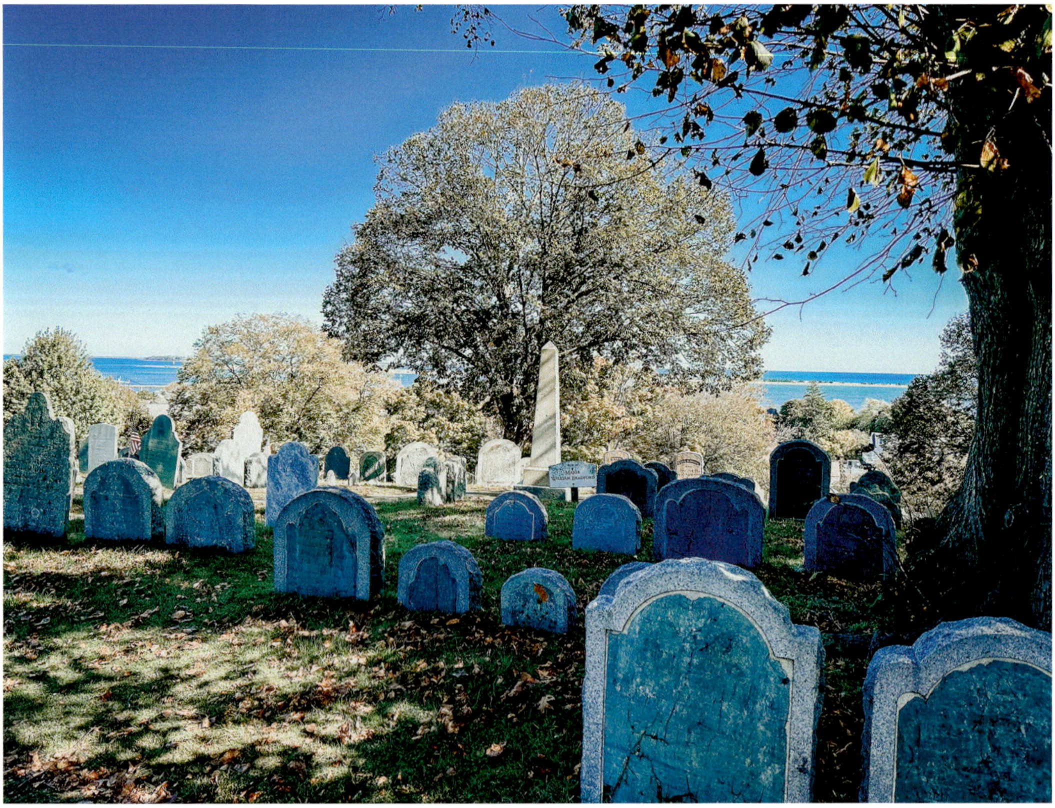

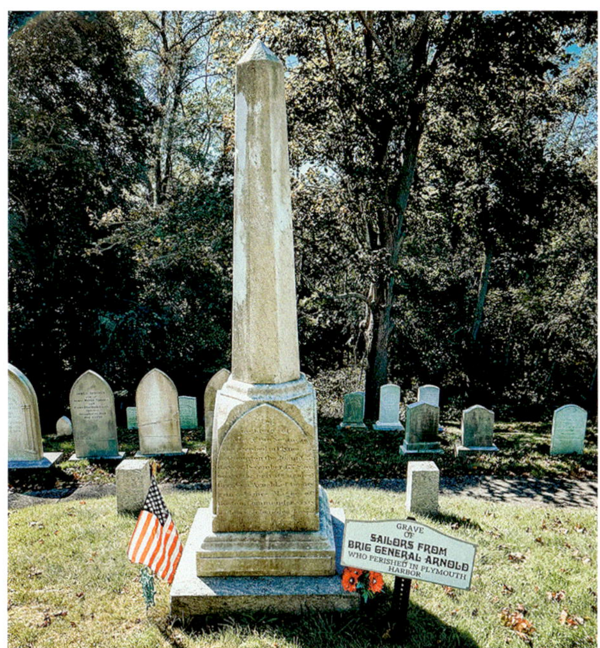

This marker stands at the site of the mass grave resulting from the shipwreck in Plymouth Harbor.

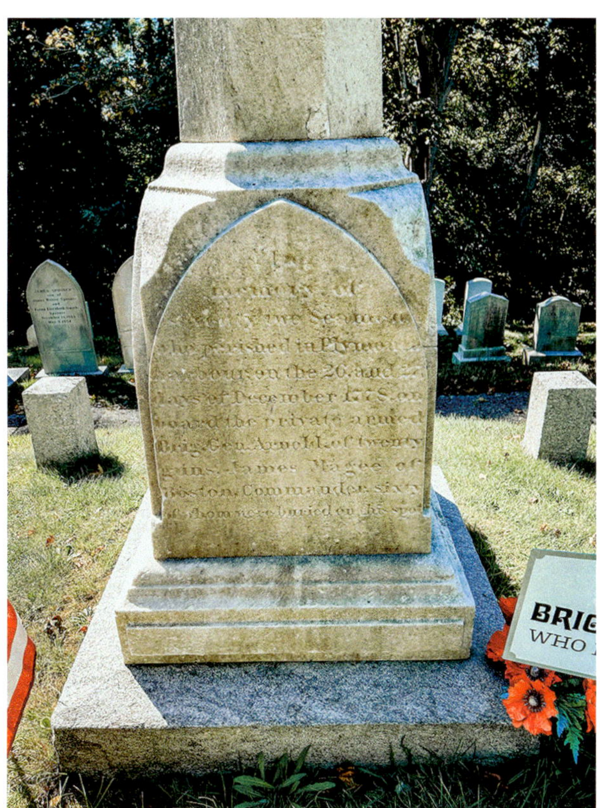

 "In memory of seventy two seamen who perished in Plymouth Harbor on the 26 and 27 days of December 1778 on board the private armed Brig. Gen. Arnold of twenty guns, numbering in officers and crew one hundred and six persons in all, James Magee, of Boston, Commander, sixty of whom were buried on this spot, and twelve in other parts of the hill."

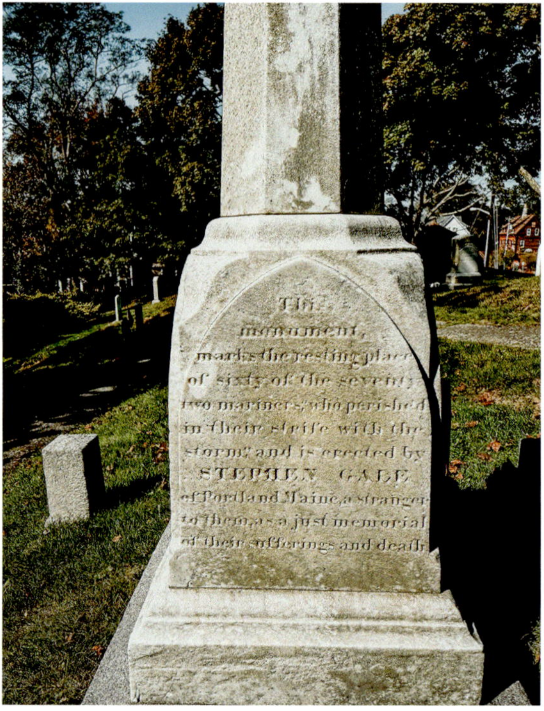

"This monument marks the resting place of sixty of the seventy two mariners who perished in their strife with the storm, and is erected by Stephen Gale, of Portland, Maine, a stranger to them, as a just memorial of their suffering and death."

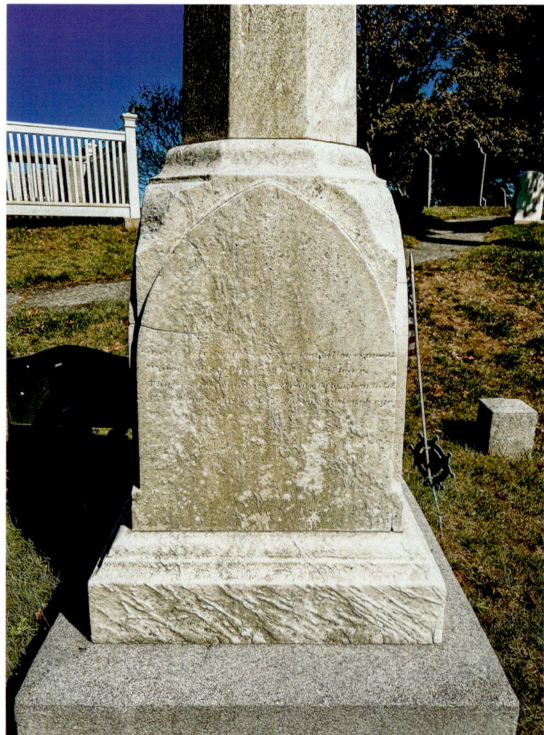

"Oh! falsely flattering were yon billows smooth, when forth, elated, sailed in evil hour that vessel, whose disastrous fate, when told, filled every breast with sorrow and each eye with piteous tears."

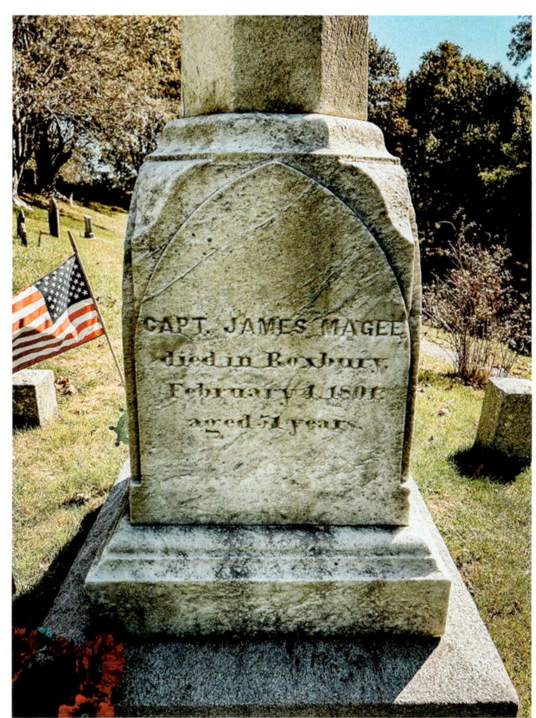

"Capt. James Magee died in Roxbury, February 4, 1801, aged 51 years."

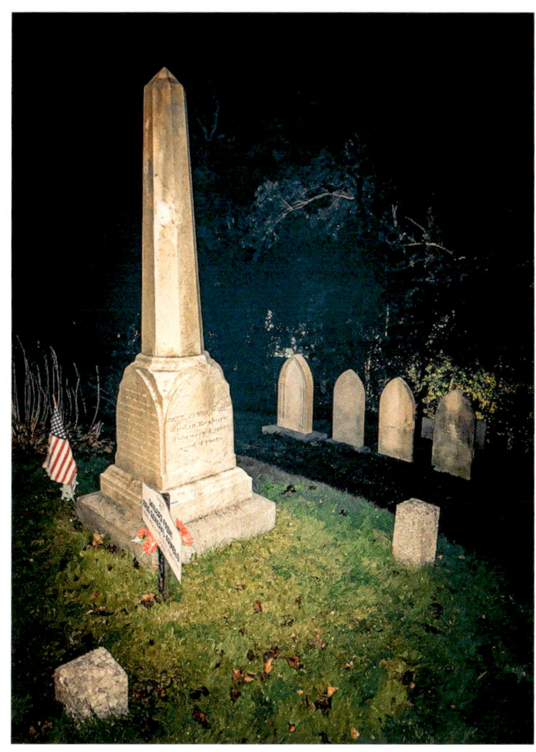

This photo was taken at the mass grave of the sailors of the *General Arnold* at night.

Unlike the grave of William Bradford, the grave of Zabdiel Sampson is rather unassuming. It sits towards the bottom of Burial Hill among the other Sampson family graves and is a little hard to read due to its age. Because of this, many might not be aware of Zabdiel's importance to the state of Massachusetts. Did you know Massachusetts is one of the top states in the fishing industry, behind Alaska? Part of that may be thanks to Zabdiel.

Zabdiel was the oldest of nine children that were born to George and Hannah Sampson. You can see in the photo he is buried next to his sister, Caroline, who was the youngest. Sadly, she passed away when she was only twenty-two years old.

Zabdiel started his working life as a blacksmith, but then made a complete turn, going to Brown University and becoming a lawyer. In 1816, he was elected to the House of Representatives. While he was in the House, Zabdiel worked for legislation that would give tax breaks to fishermen, subsequently growing that industry in the state of Massachusetts. He stayed there until 1820; at this time, President Monroe made him the Collector of Customs in Plymouth.

In his personal life he married Ruth Lobdell on August 25, 1804. They had ten children together: Milton, Eudora, Algernon, Marcia, Maria Louisa, Algernon, Ruth, Zabdiel, then twins Judith and Nancy. The first son they named Algernon was born in 1809, passing away on July 15, 1815. Just ten days later, they had another little boy, who they named Algernon after their brother who had just passed. They would also lose their son Milton when he was less than a year old; he was their only child at that time.

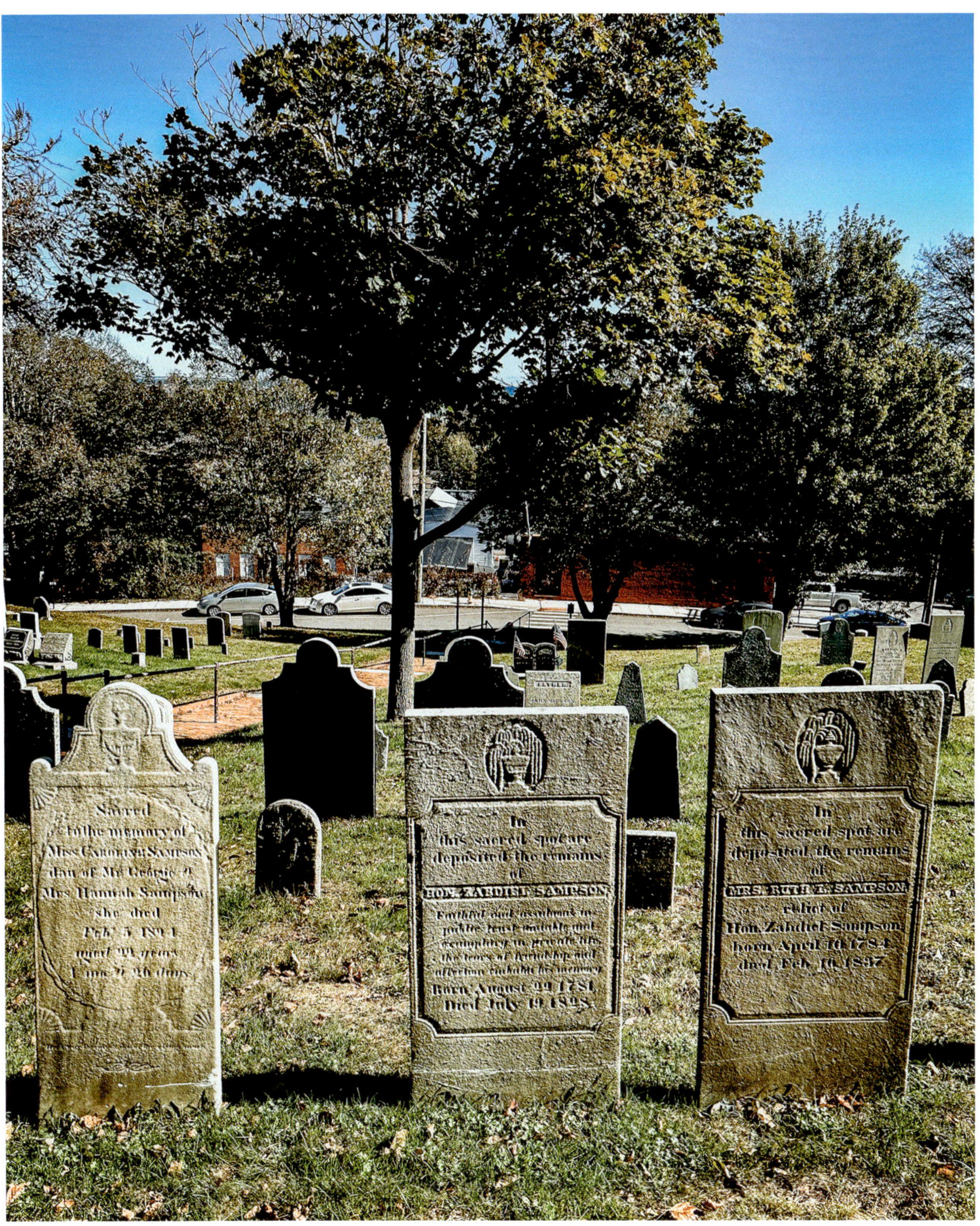

This row of graves belongs to the Sampson family; these are Caroline, Zabdiel, and Ruth specifically. Caroline's grave reads, "Sacred to the memory of Miss Caroline Sampson, dau of Mr. George & Mrs. Hannah Sampson. She died February 5, 1824, aged 22 years, 1 mo & 26 days." Zabdiel's reads, "In this sacred spot are deposited the remains of Hon. Zabdiel Sampson. [cannot read] Born August 22, 1781, Died July 19, 1828." Ruth's reads, "In this sacred spot are deposited the remains of Mrs. Ruth L. Sampson, relic of Hon. Zabdiel Sampson. Born April 10, 1784. Died Feb 10, 1837."

3

$\mathcal{F}$AMILIES OF $\mathcal{P}$LYMOUTH

The Brigham Family

Antipas Brigham and Mercy Morton were both born in 1800; he was born in Maine while she was born in Plymouth. At some point, he moved to Plymouth, and they were wed there on May 12, 1825. Their first child, a daughter named Mercy, was born September 10, 1826. She wouldn't see her first birthday as she died June 15, 1827. A little over a year later, on August 10, 1827, they had their son, Antipas. Then, on February 16, 1830, they had another daughter named Mercy (though some family trees have her as Mary).

Antipas Sr. died on August 6, 1832, leaving Mercy a widow with a four- and two-year-old. Probate records show an "insolvent estate," meaning what he had to his name when he died wasn't enough to pay off debts that he had. They ended up having to sell the family land.

Mercy never remarried and census records show her living with her younger sister, Betsy, when they were both older; their mother was living with them as well. It doesn't appear that Betsy ever married. It's possible that Mercy and her children lived with her sister after her husband's death, but there are no records to officially support this theory.

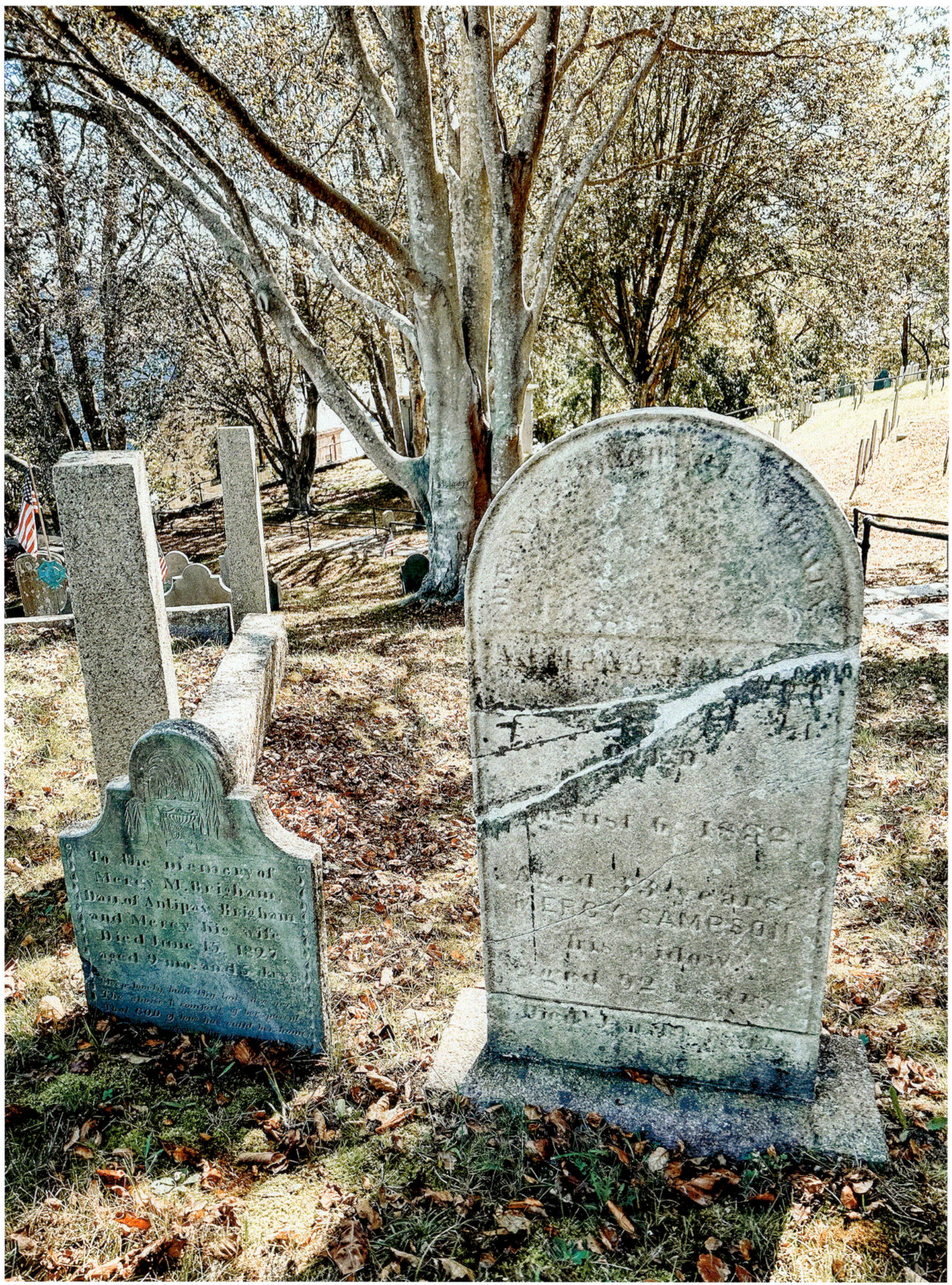

To the left is the grave of Mercy Brigham, daughter of Antipas and Mercy. To the right is the grave of her parents, which has been repaired after a break.

The Cooper Family

The story of the Cooper family is one of early loss as well as many overlapping names. Captain Joseph Cooper was born July 1, 1769; his wife, born Lucy Taylor, was born November 19, 1772. They married in Plymouth on May 28, 1791, and had eight children together. They had two sets of children with the same name: two named George and two named Lucy. The first George was born in 1793 but died in 1795. They had another boy in 1797, naming him George as well. Their first daughter was a little girl named Lucy, though she died in 1803 when she was eighteen months old. Their next child in 1805, another daughter, was named Lucy. She lived until November 25, 1889.

Joseph's younger brother, John, suffered a similar heartache in 1803. His daughter, Esther, died September 9, 1803, when she was just over two years old. Ten days later is when Joseph's daughter, Lucy, passed away.

In a tie back to one of the previously mentioned families, Joseph's older sister, Hannah, married George Sampson in 1779. Her oldest son was Zabdiel Sampson, who I previously shared was in the House of Representatives in the chapter on historical graves.

Lucy lived until October 13, 1842, when she was sixty-nine years old; Joseph died November 11, 1851, when he was eighty-two. Their second Lucy never married or had children. She lived in Plymouth until November 25, 1889, when she died.

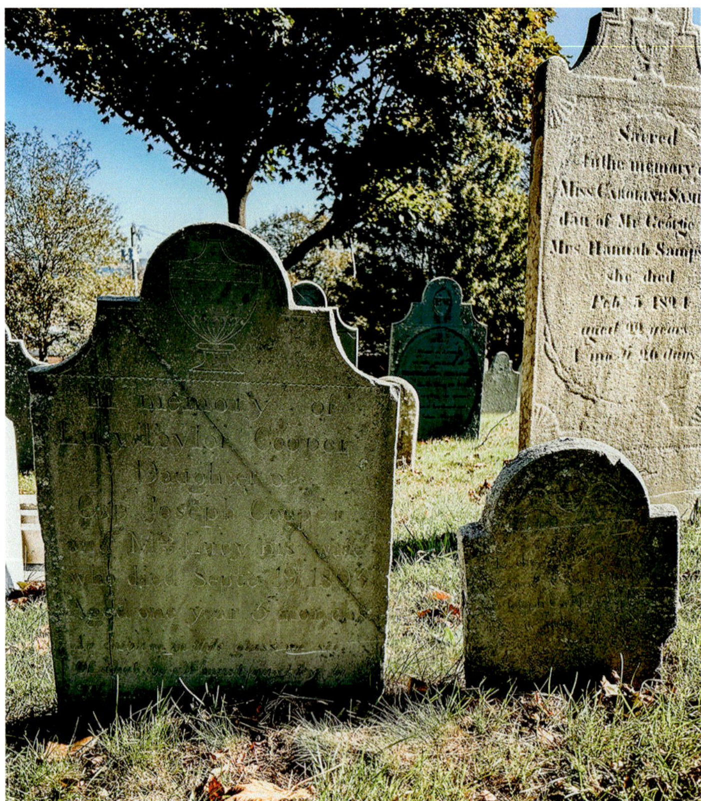

These graves belong to the Cooper family's "firsts." On the left is Lucy Taylor Cooper, who died September 19, 1803, when she was only eighteen months old. To the right is George Cooper who died November 7, 1795, just a few weeks after his second birthday. Their parents would go on to have more children, two of whom were named Lucy and George.

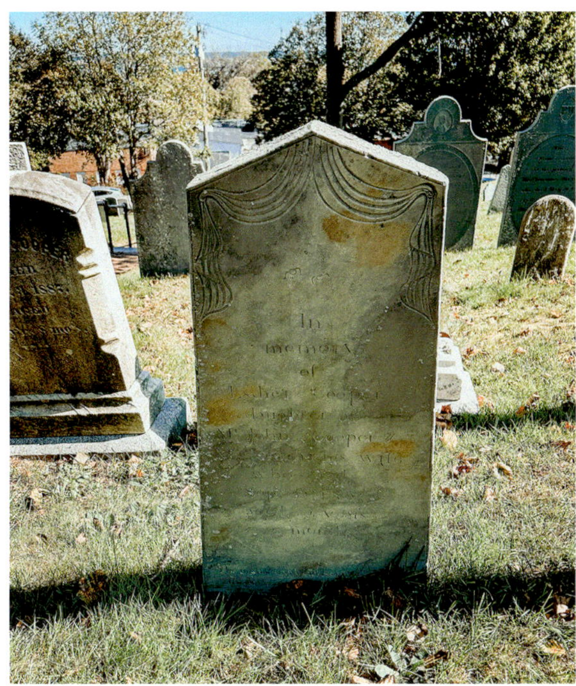

"In memory of Esther Cooper, daughter of Mr. John Cooper & Mrs. Jerusha his wife, who died Sept. 9th 1803, aged 2 years, 2 months."

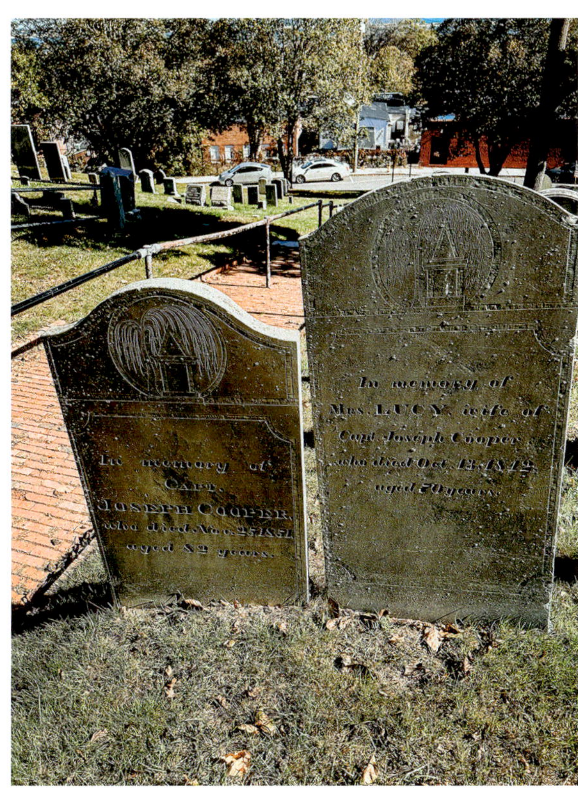

These graves belong to parents Captain Joseph Cooper (left) and Mrs. Lucy Cooper (right).

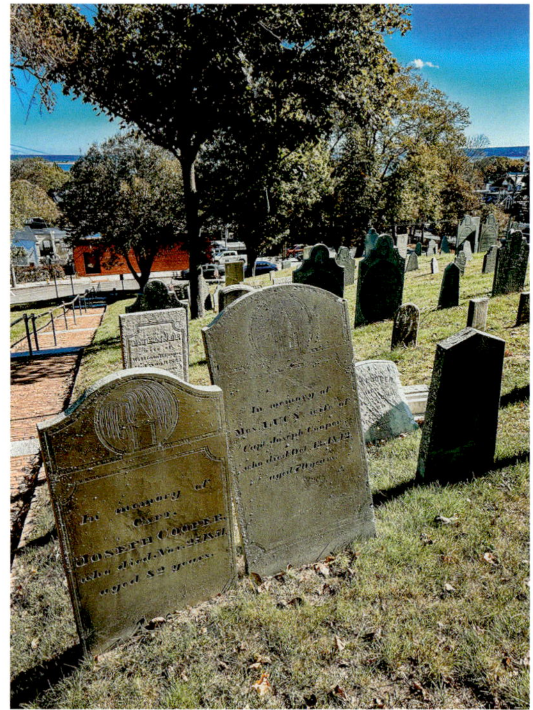

This photo shows part of where the Cooper family plot rests, near the stairs on the eastern end of the cemetery.

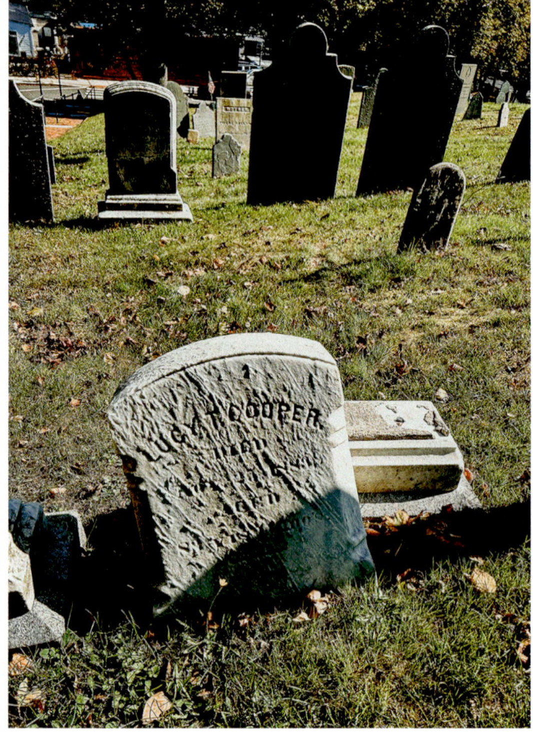

This is the Cooper family's second Lucy, whose grave is sadly broken. She lived well into adulthood, passing away when she was eighty-three.

The Goodwin Family

Captain Lewis Goodwin married his wife, Anna, on November 19, 1804. They had six children, many with similar names: Anna Lewis, Lewis, Lucia Ann, Horatio, Isabella, and Lorenzo. Sadly, Anna, Lewis, and Lorenzo didn't see their first birthdays. Anna was almost four months old when she died, while Lewis appears to be stillborn; Lorenzo had just turned two months old when he died.

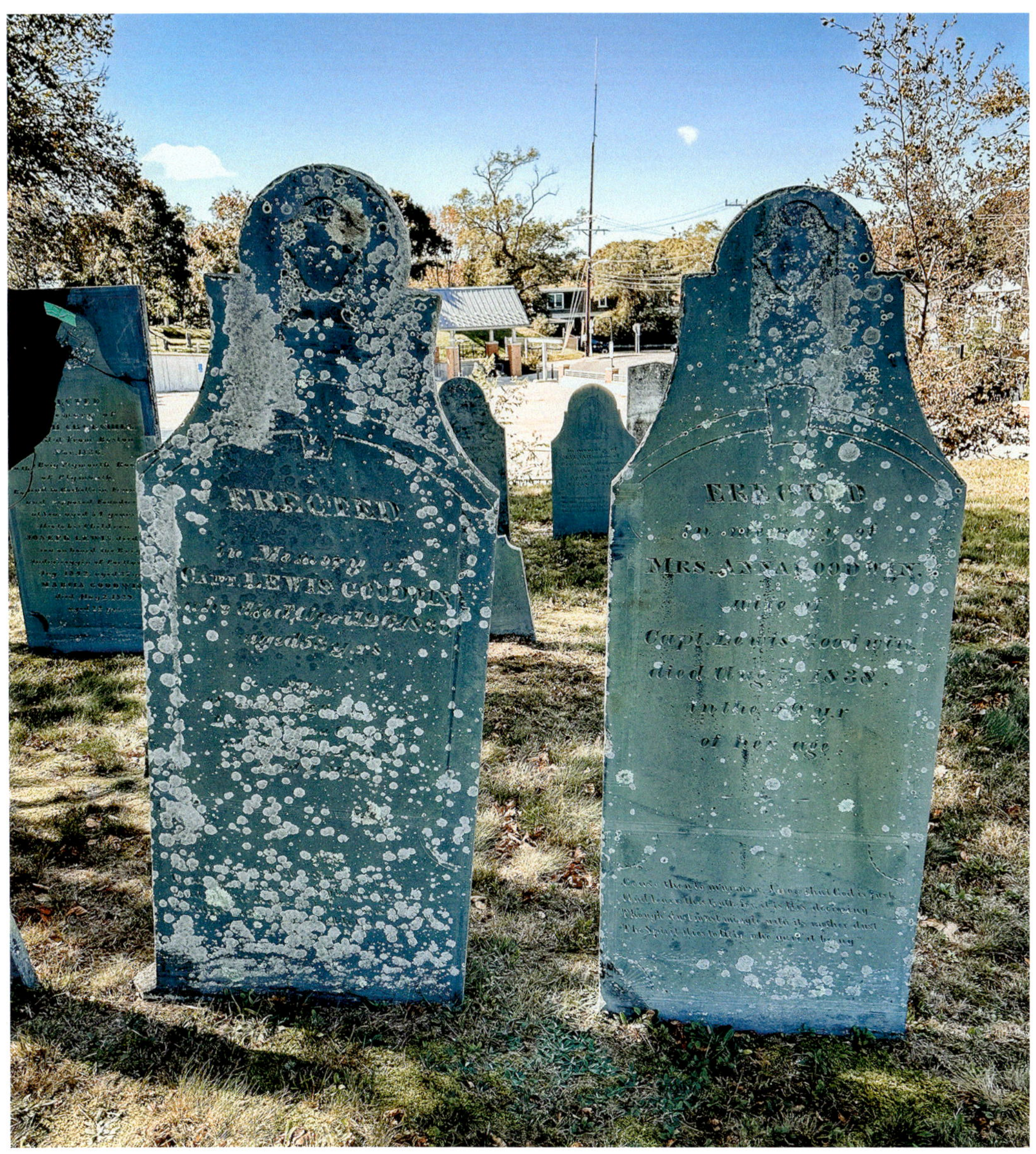

These graves belong to Captain Lewis Goodwin (left) and Mrs. Anna Goodwin (right).

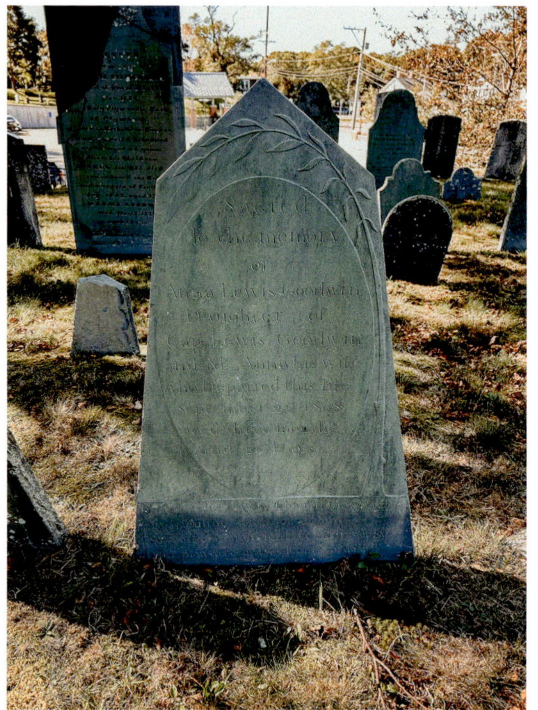

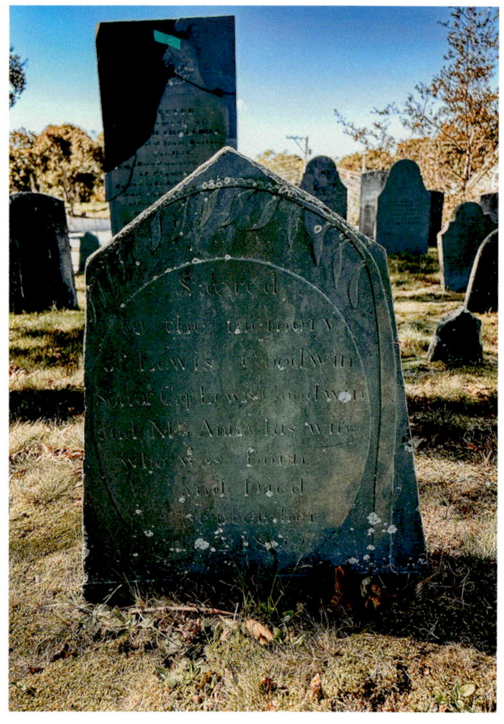

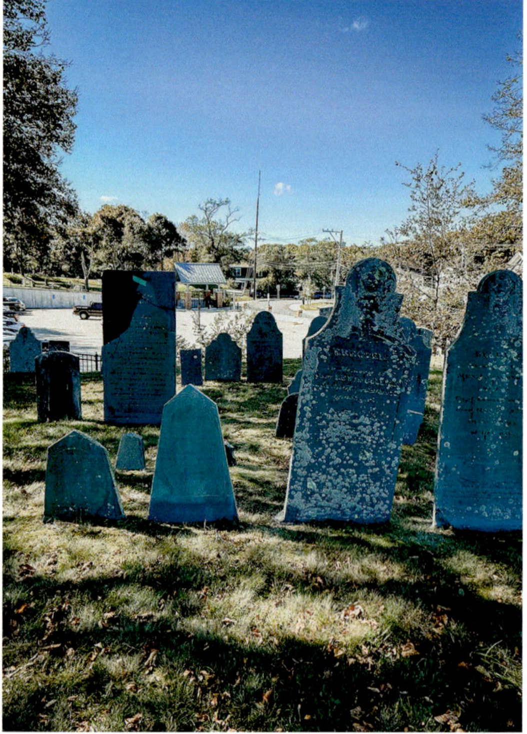

Above left: "Sacred to the memory of Anna Lewis Goodwin, daughter of Capt Lewis Goodwin and Mrs. Anna his wife, who departed this life September 26, 1808 aged 3 months and 26 days."

Above right: "Sacred to the memory of Lewis Goodwin, son of Capt Lewis Goodwin and Mrs. Anna his wife, who was born and died September 2, 1809."

Left: This photo shows little Lewis and Anna buried alongside their parents and namesakes.

The Hedge Family

Barnabas Hedge was born on December 27, 1704, to parents John and Thankful Hedge. He was the third of seven children and appears to be named after his maternal grandfather. His future wife, Mercy Barnes, was born to parents William and Alice on December 19, 1708. Alice's maiden name was Bradford; Mercy was William Bradford's great-granddaughter.

Mercy first married Samuel Cole on November 14, 1728, but she was widowed in 1731. She and Samuel had three children together: James, Ephraim, and Samuel Jr. Sadly, two of their children would die in infancy. James lived from September 12, 1729, to December 10 of that same year. Ephraim lived from November 14, 1730, to January 25, 1731. Samuel Sr. would die August 18, 1731, and little Samuel wasn't born until November of that year. This means, after losing two children, Mercy was widowed while she was still pregnant.

Mercy then married Barnabas on December 21, 1733. They had between seven and nine children together. I say this because there are nine children listed on most family trees, but there aren't any birth or death records, which makes me think they may have been stillborn. A lot of stillbirths were still recorded though, so it's hard to say for sure.

Their children were Mercy, Lemuel, Abigail, Barnabas Jr., Lemuel, Lothrop, and Sarah; the children "in question" were named John and William. In her new marriage, Mercy was still no stranger to losing her children. Both Lemuels died young, with the first living September 20, 1736, to October 3; the second lived from June 25, 1742, until July 7. Lothrop, born November 5, 1744, would pass away January 20, 1745.

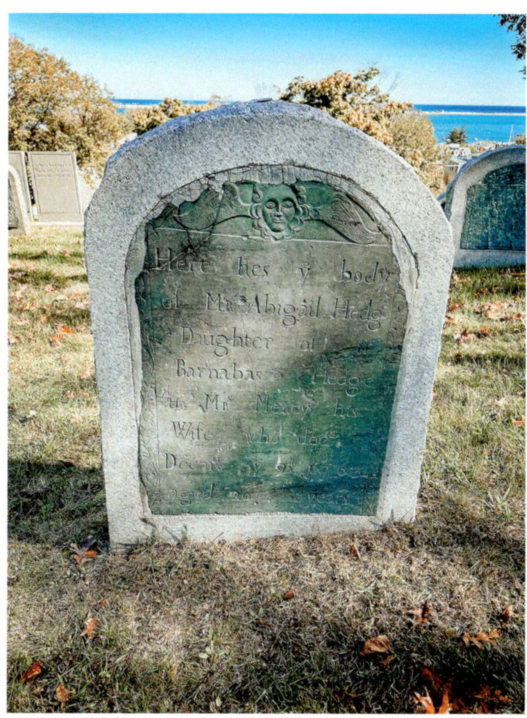

"Here lies ye body of Mrs. Abigail Hedge, daughter of Mr. Barnabas Hedge and Mrs. Mercy his wife, who dec'd. Decm. ye 9th, 1763, aged 26 years."

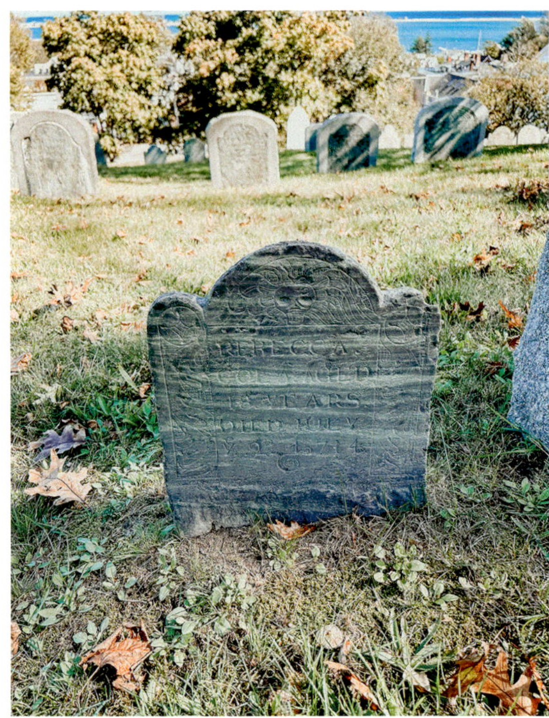

"Rebecca Cole, aged 18 years, died July ye 2nd, 1714." Rebecca was the sister of Samuel Cole, the first husband of Mercy Hedge. She was born in 1696 to Ephraim and Rebecca Cole as the oldest of four siblings.

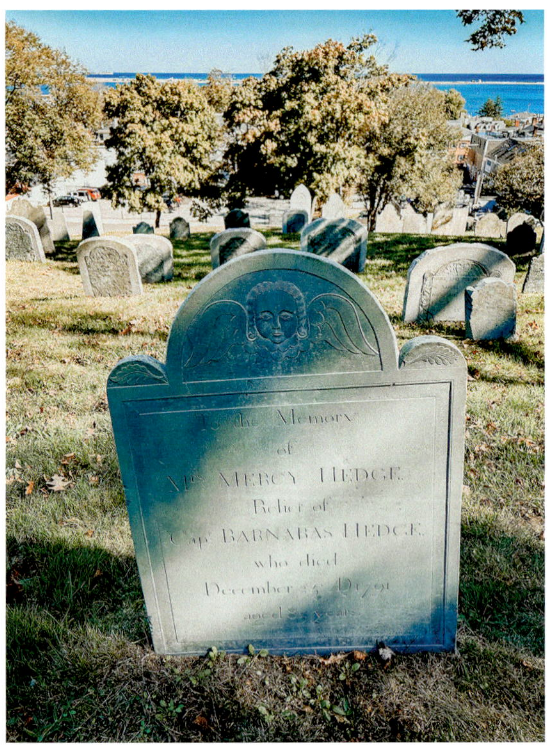

"To the memory of Mrs. Mercy Hedge, relict of Capt. Barnabas Hedge, who died December 25, AD 1791, aged 83 years."

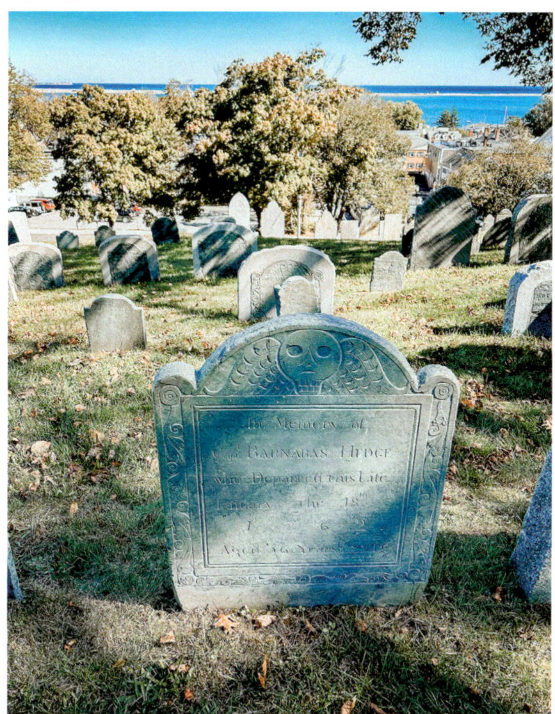

"In memory of Capt. Barnabas Hedge,
who departed this life January the 18th
1762, aged 56 years and 22 days."
It feels very fitting to have a view
of the bay from a captain's grave.

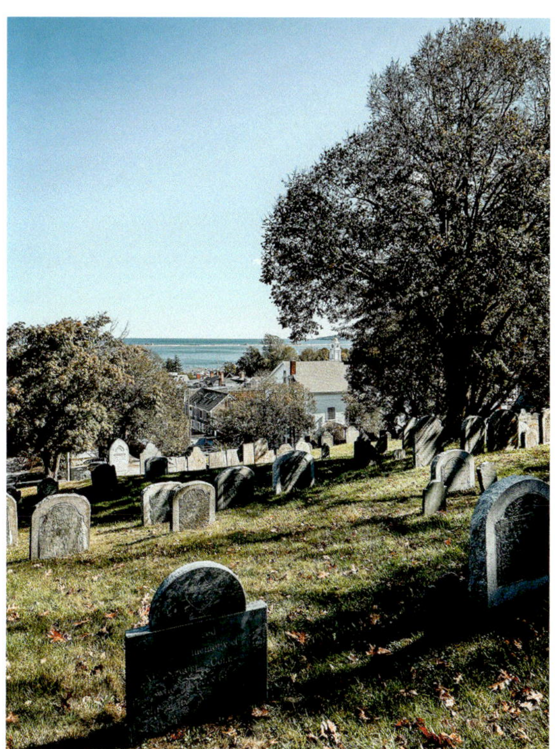

The front left stone belongs to Samuel
Cole, who was the half-brother of
Abigail Hedge from their mother's
first marriage. He was named after his
father who died before he was born.

The Howland Family

During a lot of cemetery strolls, there are certain graves that I feel particularly drawn to. In my book about Colonial Park Cemetery in Savannah, GA, I explain a lot of detail on how I was drawn to the grave of Isabella Chadbourn and felt compelled to research her. For Burial Hill in Plymouth, the grave of Hannah Howland was that grave. She was so young when she died, only twenty-six, and her epitaph simply notes that she, "died of a languishment."

Hannah was born June 11, 1753 to parents Consider and Ruth. She was the youngest of fifteen children. Her siblings were Lucy, Elizabeth, Ruth, Mary, Thomas, Consider, Joanna, Martha, Joseph, Bethiah, Consider, Experience, John, and Joseph. Their father, Consider Sr., died when Hannah was only six years old; their mother never remarried. Hannah died on January 25, 1780.

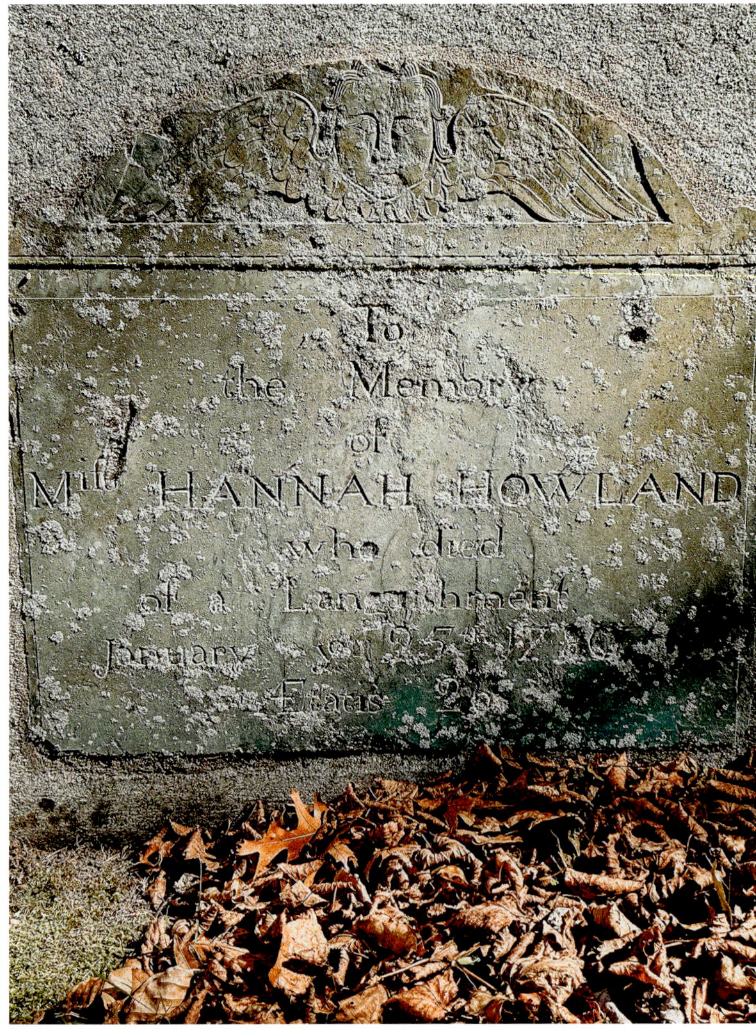

"To the memory of Miss Hannah Howland, who died of a languishment, January ye 25th, 1780, age 26."

Hannah had two older brothers named Joseph and two named Consider, after their father. The first Joseph was born February 20, 1742; he only lived until May 11 of that year. The second Joseph was a twin, with the boys being born August 2, 1751. While this Joseph would live to adulthood, his twin, John, wouldn't be so lucky. He passed away on August 30, just four weeks after being born. The first Consider lived from 1736–1743. The second was born in 1745 and like Joseph before him, would also live to adulthood.

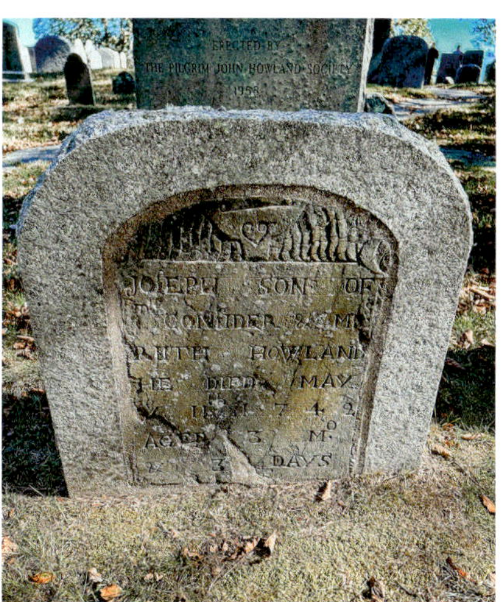

Right: "Joseph, son of Mr. Consider & Mrs. Ruth Howland. He died May ye 11th, 1742 aged 3 months and 3 days."

Below: At the center of this photo you can see an American flag at the grave of Joseph Howland, 1751–1806. He was the older brother of Hannah, who I continue to mention throughout the section on the Howland family.

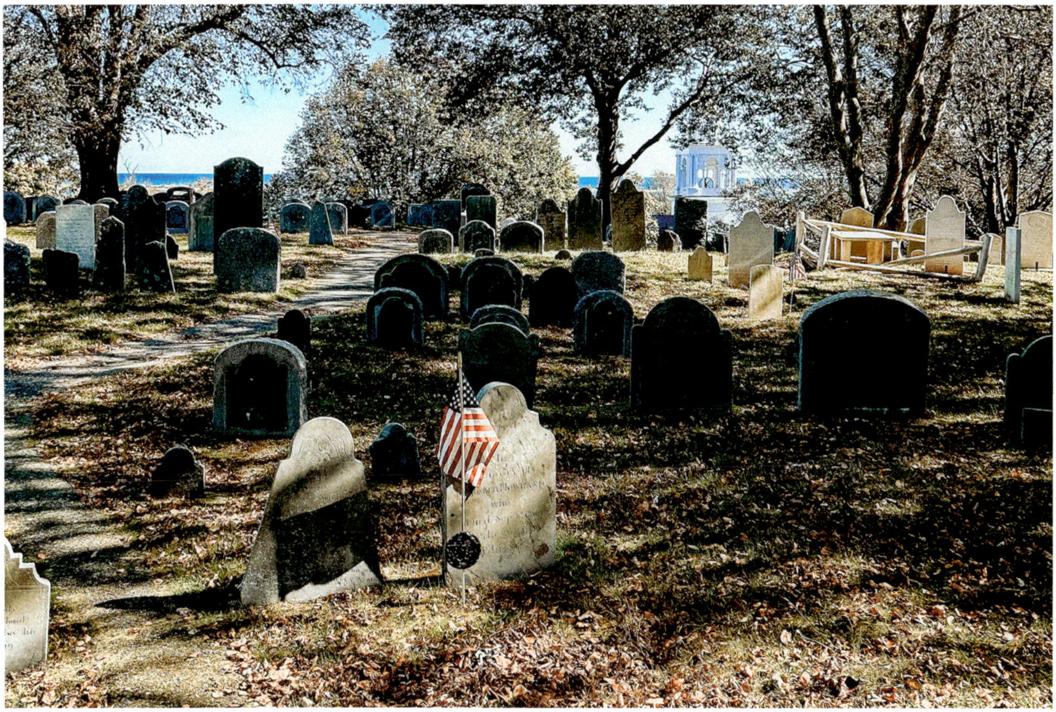

Hannah's older sister, Lucy, would go on to marry Abraham Hammatt and have three children with him: Lucy, William, and Abraham. Abraham Jr., born in 1750, married a woman named Priscilla on November 26, 1774. They would also have three children: William, Sophia and Elizabeth. Sadly, Abraham and his daughter, Sophia, would die the same year from "malignant fever." Abraham died October 13, 1797, and Sophia died December 1; she was only thirteen. The father and daughter duo are buried together and noted on the same headstone.

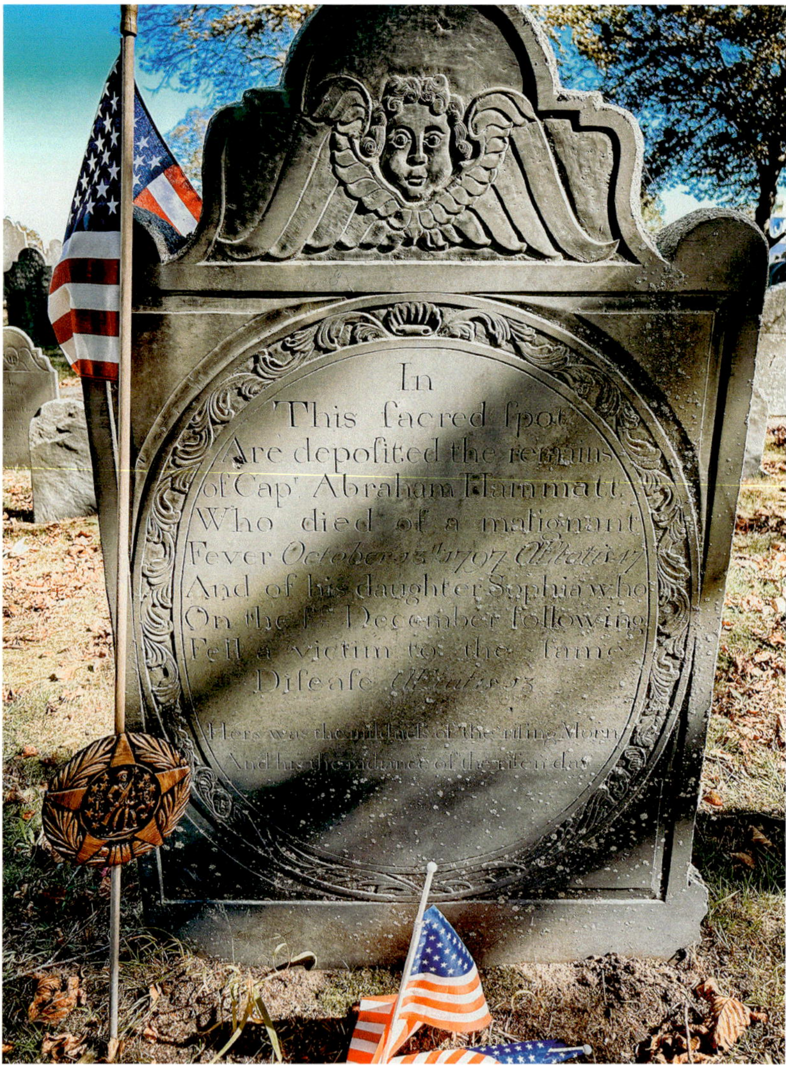

"In This sacred spot are deposited the remains of Capt Abraham Hammatt, who died of a malignant fever, October 13th 1797 Ætatis 47. And of his daughter Sophia who, on the 1st December following fell a victim to the same Disease Ætatis 13.Hers was the mildness of the rising morn, and his the radiance of the risen day."

The Howland family is one of the oldest settling families in Plymouth. Hannah and her siblings are the great-great grandchildren of John Howland, who was born in England between 1592 and 1602 (some records and family trees vary). His parents were Henry and Margaret Howland. John crossed the Atlantic on the *Mayflower* in 1620. He's noted to have fallen overboard during the voyage, though they managed to save him. He married Elizabeth Tilley on August 14, 1623.

Elizabeth came over on the *Mayflower* with her own family but was orphaned after that first winter when her parents, aunt, and uncle all died. It is noted that Elizabeth could "excel her associates" as she was able to write her own name. It's thought that John is the one who taught her how to do that, which would be very unusual for that time. After marrying John, they had ten children: Desire, John, Hope, Elizabeth, Lydia, Hannah, Joseph, Jabez, Ruth and Isaac. We can trace Hannah's lineage through his son, Joseph.

After that initial mishap on the Mayflower, John Howland ended up being the longest surviving male from the ship. He died February 23, though even his epitaph isn't clear on the year, noting both 1672 and 1673.

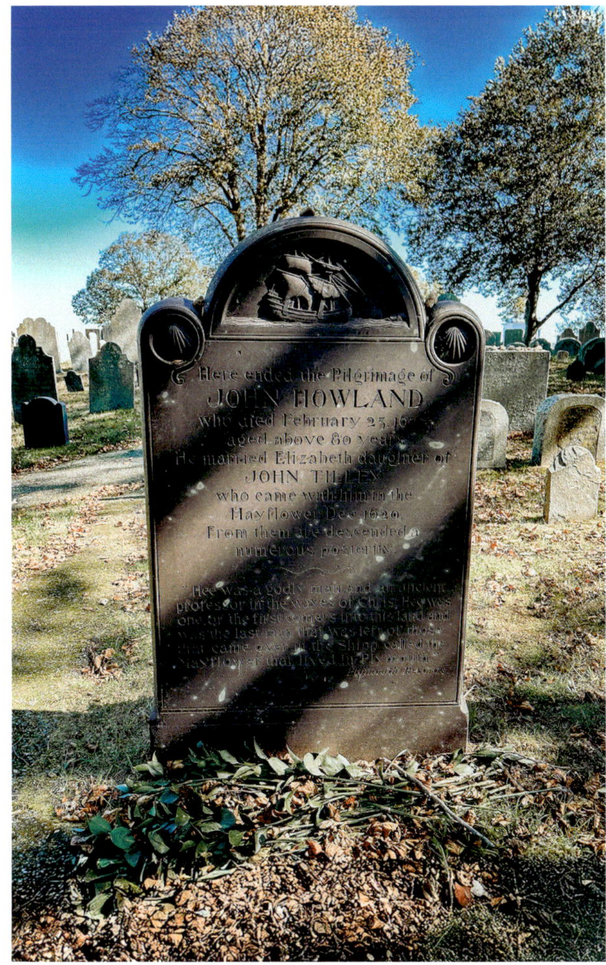

"Here ended the Pilgrimage of John Howland, who died February 23, 1672/3, aged above 80 years. He married Elizabeth, daughter of John Tilley who came with him in the Mayflower Dec. 1620. From them are descended a numerous posterity. He was a godly man and an ancient professor in the ways of Christ. He was one of the first comers into this land and was the last man that was left of those that came over in the Ship called the Mayflower that lived in Plymouth."

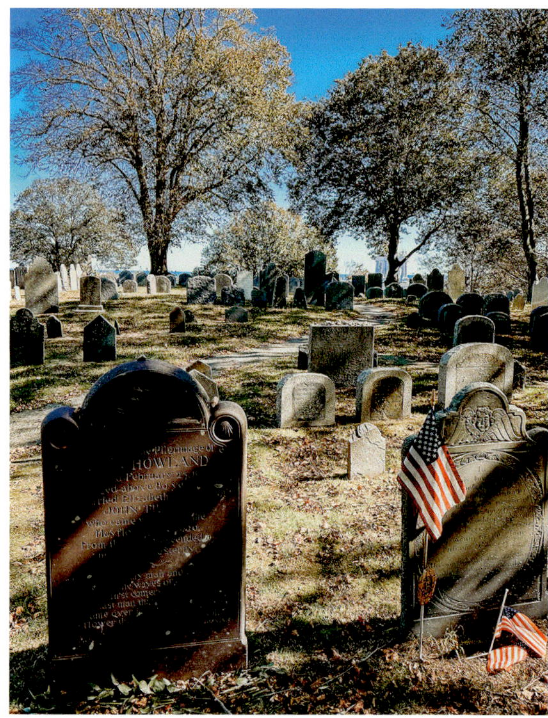

Here is John Howland and Abraham Hammatt's graves in the Howland family plot.

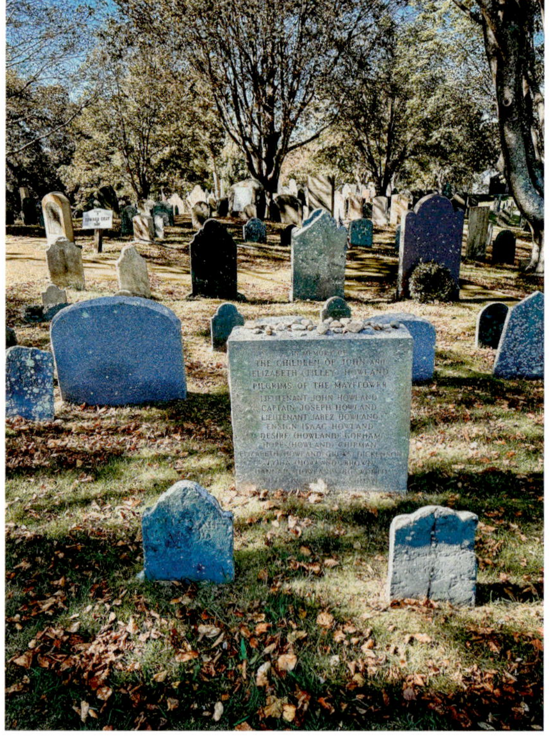

At the center of this photo is a memorial for John and Elizabeth's children: John, Joseph, Jabez, Isaac, Desire, Hope, Elizabeth, Lydia, Hannah, and Ruth.

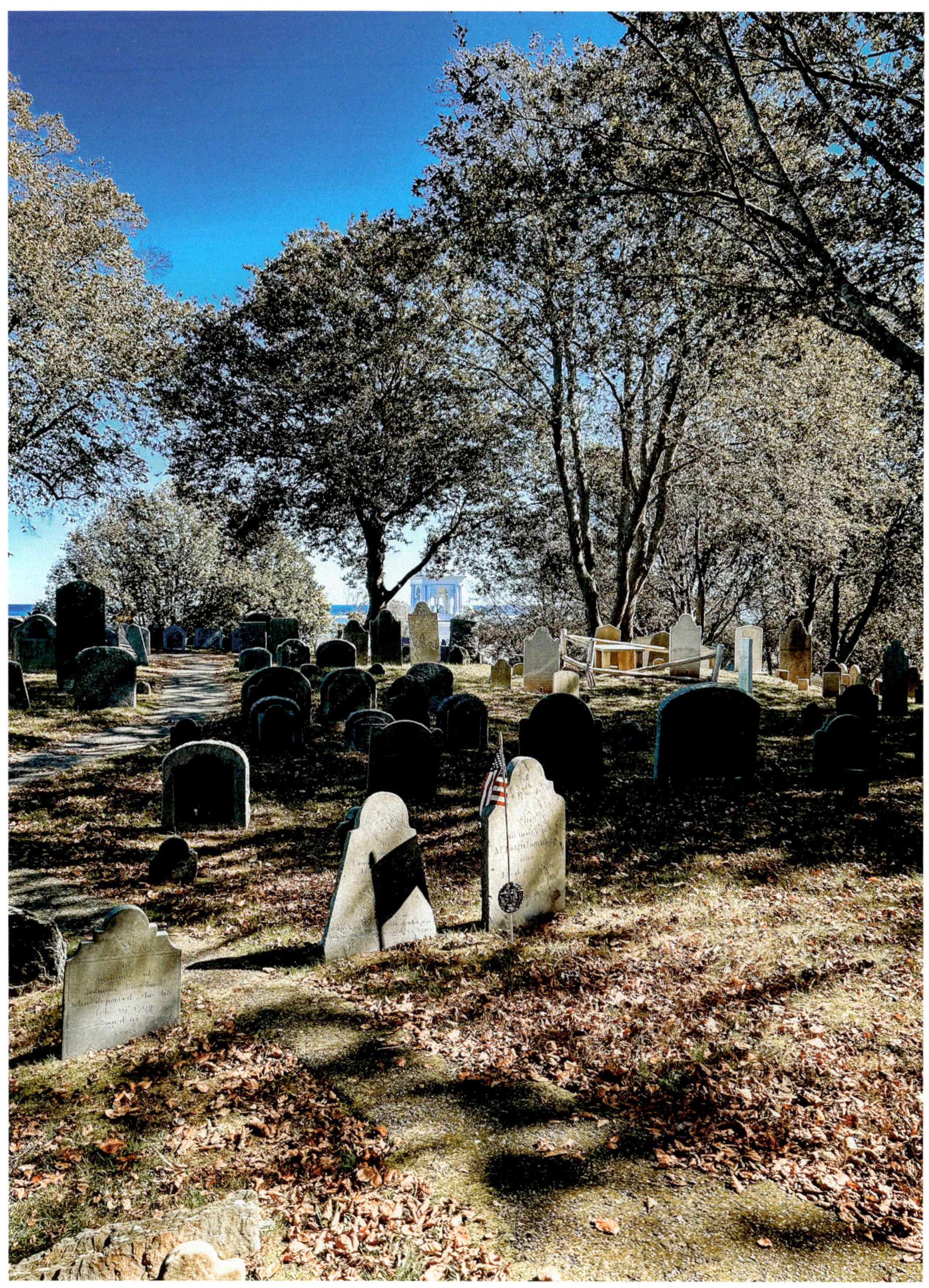

More of the Howland family graves can be seen here.

The LeBaron Family

The LeBaron family has quite an interesting origin story. Francis LeBaron came to Massachusetts from France in 1694. He was the doctor onboard a French privateer that was shipwrecked; everyone on board was taken prisoner. While being held in Plymouth, the people in the town saw him performing surgery. As they were without a town doctor at the time, they successfully petitioned for his pardon.

He would marry Mary Wilder the following year on September 6, 1695. They went on to have three sons together: James, Lazarus, and Francis. Francis Sr. died when he was only thirty-six on August 8, 1704. Mary would remarry in 1707 to a man named Return Waite, but they never had children together.

Lazarus LeBaron would follow in his father's footsteps as the town doctor. He first married Lidia Bartlett on May 16, 1720, and they had seven children: Lazarus, Joseph, Lydia, Mary, Hannah, Teresa, and Bartlett. Both Lazarus Jr. and Joseph would be doctors as well, making the LeBarons Plymouth's resident physicians for generations. Lidia died in 1742 and, with many children to care for, he remarried on May 2, 1743, to Lydia Bradford, another of William Bradford's great-granddaughters. They also had seven children: Isaac, Elizabeth, Lemuel, Francis, William, Priscillia, and Margaret. Lazarus lived until September 2, 1773.

Isaac LeBaron, the oldest child of Lazarus's second marriage, was born January 25, 1743. He married into the Howland family by marrying Martha Howland December 1, 1744; Martha was the older sister of Hannah. They had four children together: Isaac, Martha, Francis, and Mary.

Lazarus's younger brother, and their father's namesake, Francis, was born June 13, 1701. He married Sarah Bartlett on November 23, 1721. He likely met her through Lazarus; his first wife, Lidia, was Sarah's sister. Francis and Sarah had six children: Francis, Mary, Isaac, Sarah, an unnamed daughter, and Frances.

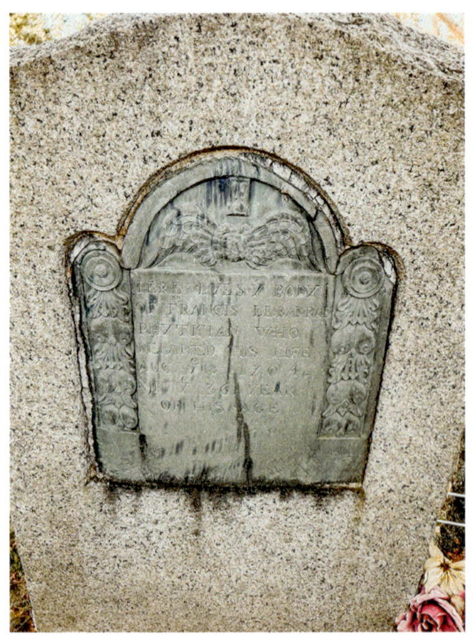

"Here lyes ye body of Mr. Francis Lebarran, physician, who departed this life Aug. ye 8th 1704 in ye 36th year of his age." You can see in the epitaph that his last name was misspelled quite badly as it's meant to be spelled "LeBaron."

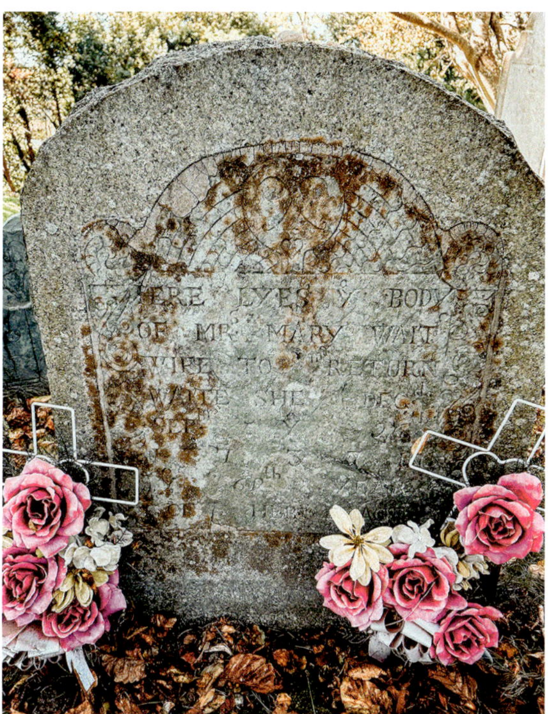

"Here lyes ye body of Mrs. Mary Waite, wife to Mr. Return Waite. She dec'd Sep'br ye 26th 1737 in ye 69th year of her age." At the grave of Mary Waite you can see where someone had recently left her flowers.

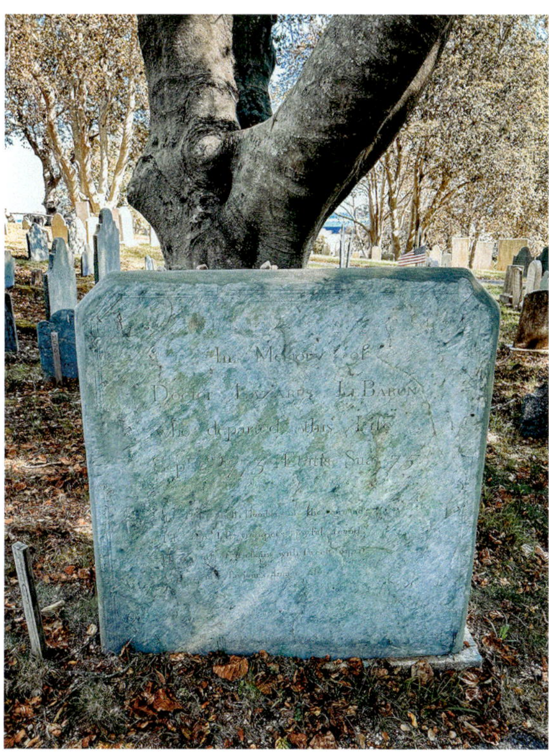

"In memory of Doctor Lazarus LeBaron, who departed this life Sep'r 2'd 1773. Etatis Saul 75. My flesh shall slumber in the ground, till the last trumpet's joyful sound; then burst the chains with sweet surprise, and in my Saviour's image rise."

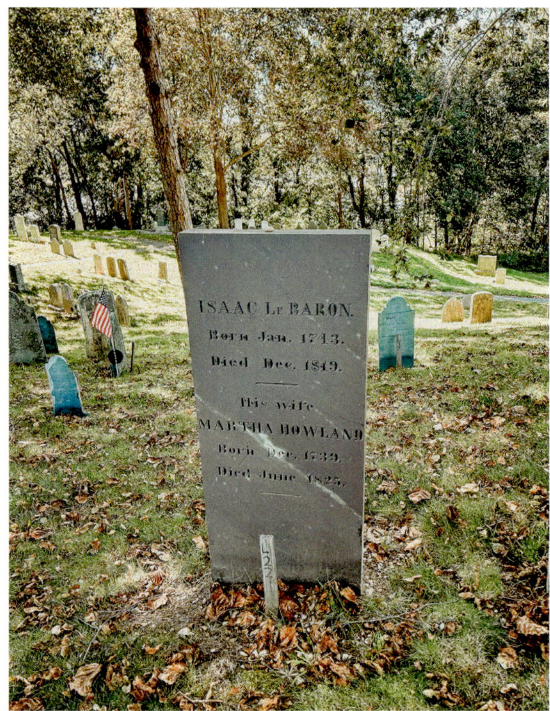

"Isaac LeBaron, born Jan. 1743, Died Dec. 1819. His wife, Martha Howland, born Dec. 1739, died June 1825."

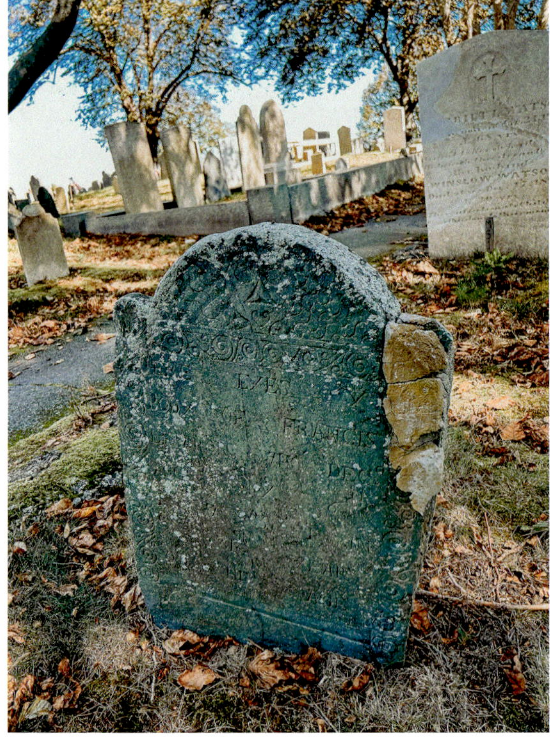

"Here lyes ye body of Francis LeBaron, who dec'd August ye 6th 1731 in ye 31st year of his age."

The Tribble Family

Joseph and Mary Tribble married February 23, 1794. They had seven children together: Thomas, Mary, Thomas, William, Hiram, Robert, and George. And while William and Robert aren't buried in Plymouth, their deaths are noted on their parents' grave.

William died when he was only twenty-three in 1827 in Port Au Prince. Joseph died a year later on March 13, 1828, when he was fifty-five. Robert died in 1832 when he was only twenty-one in Savannah, GA. I am from Savannah and unfortunately couldn't find his name or cause of death in the records I have access to. Mary died the following year on February 10 when she was fifty-five.

Joseph was the oldest of eight children born to Joseph and Sarah Tribble. His younger brother, John, was born in 1782. He married Bathsheba Holmes in Plymouth on January 14, 1804. They would have six children together: Christiana, Albert, Winslow, Gustavus, Marcia, and Lavantia. Sadly, Bathsheba died July 21, 1815, when she was only twenty-nine years old. Many of their children died young and are notated on her tombstone. Albert died in 1817 when he was only nine years old and Marcia died in 1818 when she was only four. Gustavus died in 1821 when he was nine as well, Lavantia died at age two in March 1824, and Christiana died a few months later in December when she was nineteen.

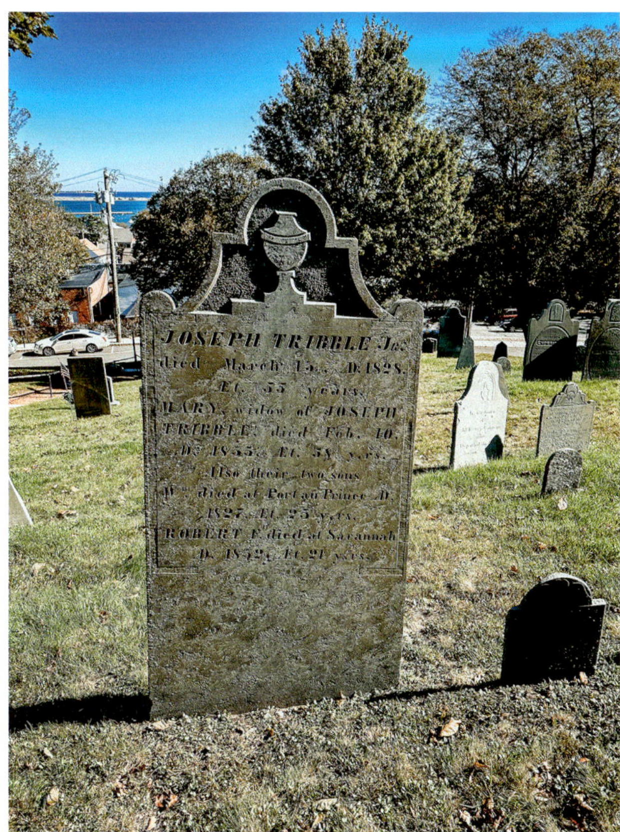

This tombstone was erected for four family members. "Joseph Tribble Jr. died March 13, 1828 aged 55 years. Mary, widow of Joseph Tribble, died February 10, 1833 aged 58 years. Also their two sons. Wm died at Port au Princes 1827 aged 25 years. Robert F. died at Savannah 1832 aged 21 years."

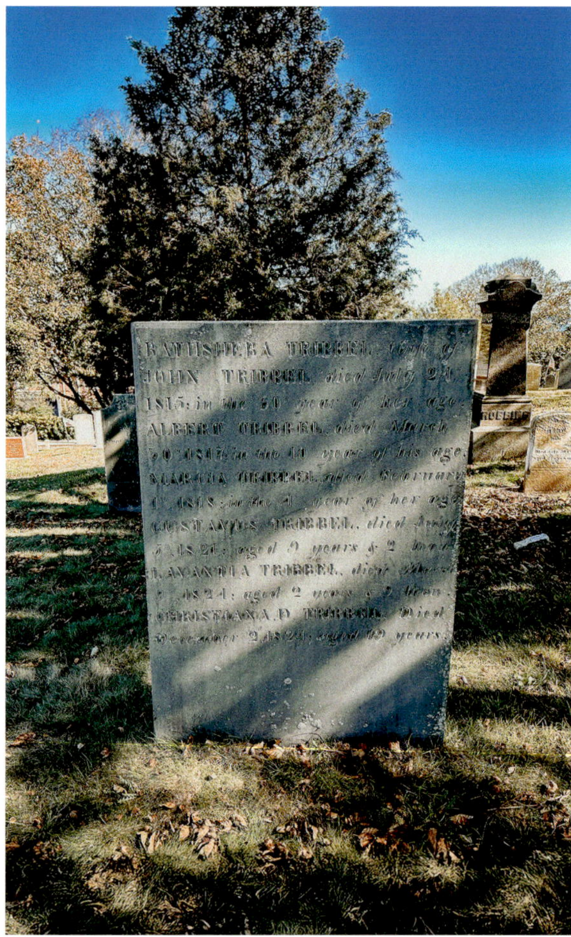

This grave marks the resting place of Bathsheba Tribble and her children Albert, Marcia, Gustavus, Lavantia, and Christiana. You can see where their last name was continuously misspelled as "Tribbel."

The Virgin Family

The story of the Virgin family is one that is all too familiar in Plymouth from this time period. John Virgin was born March 15, 1792 to parents John and Priscilla. He was the oldest of four sons, but the youngest two didn't survive childhood. He married Abigail Davie on December 14, 1816, and they had one daughter together in 1818; her name was also Abigail.

Like his father before him, John was a ship captain. He was sailing from St. Ubes (which is now Setúbal, Portugal) to Boston when he was lost at sea in October 1822. Abigail was widowed, without her husband's remains, and had a four-year-old daughter. In what I find to be an unusual circumstance of the time, Abigail never remarried, though she lived to be eighty-seven years old. A lot of widows and widowers at the time would remarry either for help with their children or for many women, security. She is buried next to John's empty grave, and I wonder now if she was waiting for him to come back.

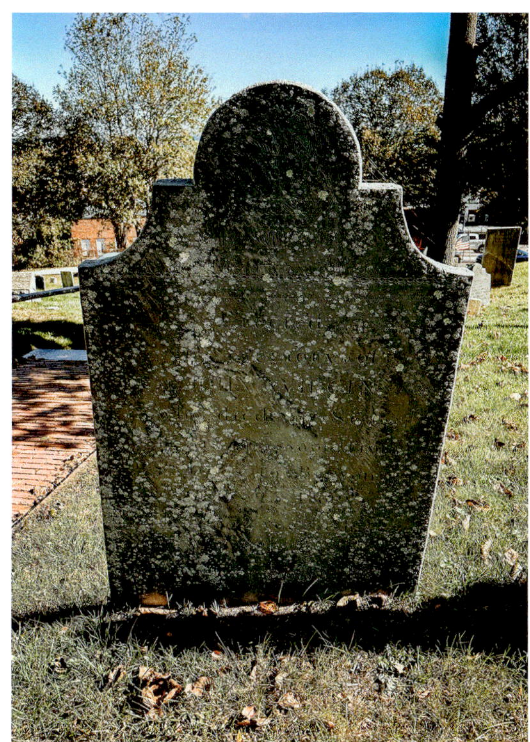

The grave of Captain John Virgin is difficult to read. The epitaph states, "Erected in memory of Cap. John Virgin, who died at sea, on his passage from St. Ubes to Boston, Oct. 23, 1822 in the 32 year of his age."

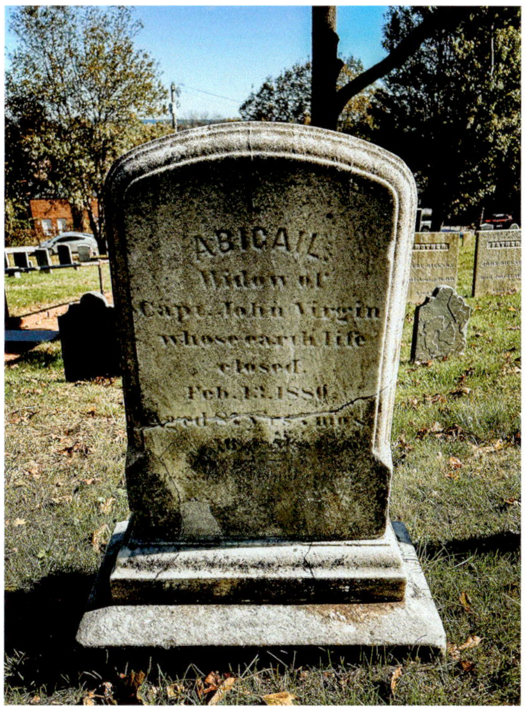

This is the grave of Abigail Virgin, John's wife. Her epitaph reads, "Abigail, widow of Capt. John Virgin, whose earth life closed Feb. 13, 1880, aged 87 years, 7 mos, 16 days. Blessed are the pure of heart." She never remarried after John's death.

4

EARLY COLONIAL LIFE IN MASSACHUSETTS

Betsy Shaw was born Elizabeth Holmes to parents Ichabod and Rebecca in 1775 as the youngest of eleven children. She married Ichabod Shaw on July 5, 1794, and they had a daughter, Elizabeth, in 1795. Their happy family life was to be short lived though as Betsy died December 26, 1795, when she was only twenty. There is no date of death given for young Elizabeth, but she was born sometime in 1795 and is noted as being buried with her mother, passing away when she was only seven months old.

Four years after Betsy's death, Ichabod would remarry Ester Holmes on December 27, 1799; she was Betsy's older sister. They don't appear to have had any children together. Ester died November 1, 1846, and Ichabod died July 26, 1837. He is buried between the two sisters.

Lemuel Brown married Sarah Palmer on December 7, 1797. They had four children together: Ann, Lemuel, Sarah (1801–1802), and Sarah (born 1804). Tragically, all their children would die young. Ann died in 1809 when she was eleven, Lemuel in 1801 when he was one, Sarah in 1802 when she was one, and Sarah in 1807 when she was four.

Sarah passed away on June 6, 1821, when she was forty-six. Lemuel remarried a woman named Ann, though the date isn't clear. They never had children and Lemuel died November 19, 1845. Ann lived almost another two years, dying January 28, 1847. Like Ichabod, Lemuel is buried between his two wives. Both men are also buried near their children that they outlived for far too long.

Joseph Churchill was born in 1782 to Thaddeus and Asenath. He would first marry Mercy Goodwin November 11, 1804. She was the mother to all his children: Joseph, Amelia, Edward, George, Marcia, and Charles. They would lose four of these children young; Amelia died when she was seven months in 1807, Edward died in 1809 at age one, George died in 1811 when he was about three months old, and Charles died in 1825 when he was three.

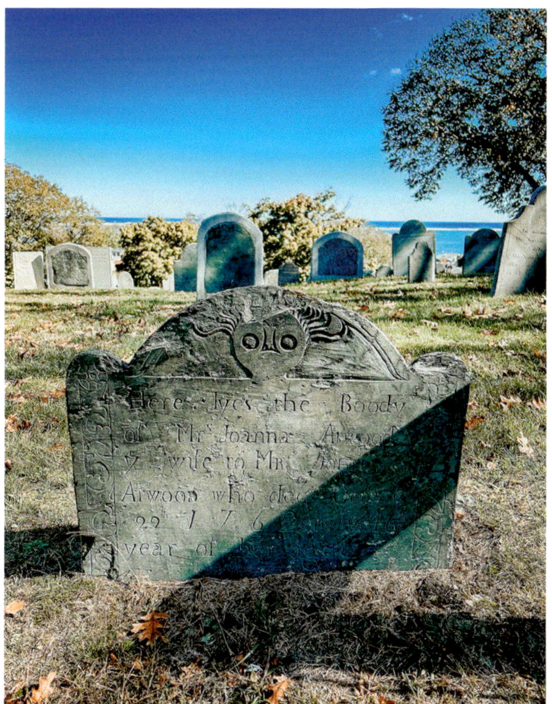

The grave of Joanna Atwood contains a misspelling, which wasn't uncommon at the time. It's not her name that's misspelled though; her epitaph reads, "Here lyes the boody" with two o's in body. Mrs. Atwood was only forty-five years old when she died.

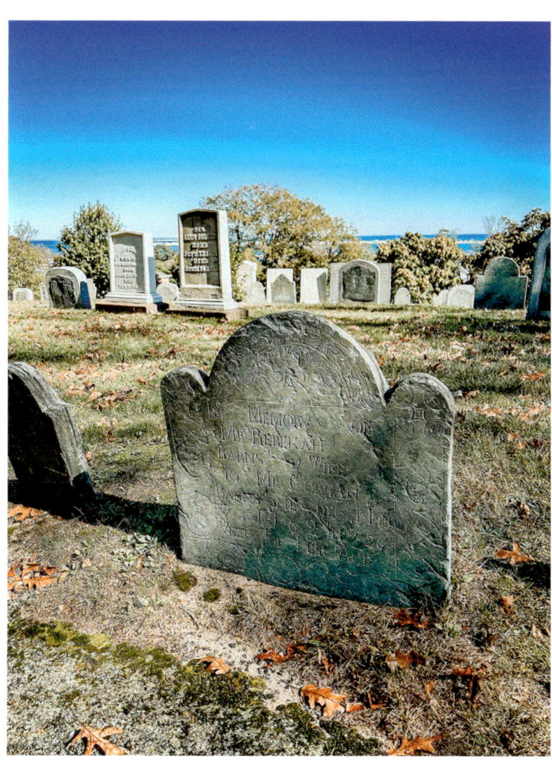

Rebekah Barnes (misspelled as Barns) was one of Joanna Atwood's daughters. She died in 1762 when she was only twenty-six.

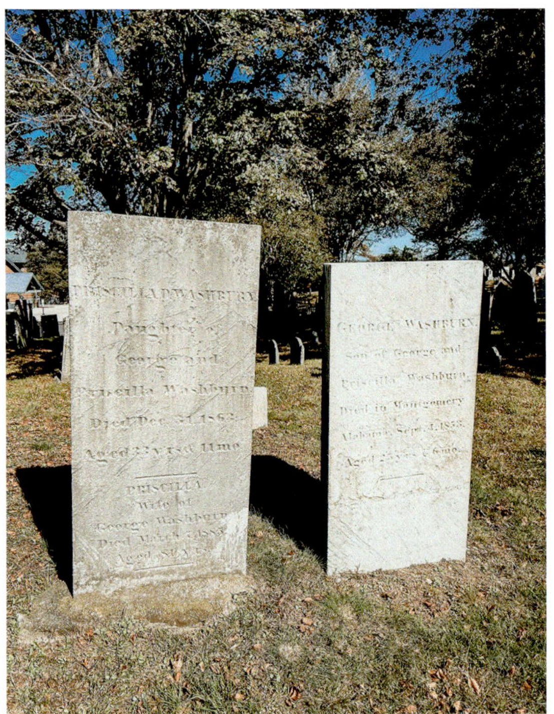

While the Washburn siblings would live to adulthood, it would not be for very long. George and Priscilla were born to parents (also named George and Priscilla) in 1828 and 1830, respectively. George died at age twenty-five in September of 1853 while in Alabama. Priscilla died when she was thirty-three on New Year's Eve in 1863; she's one of the few causes of death I could find, dying of consumption.

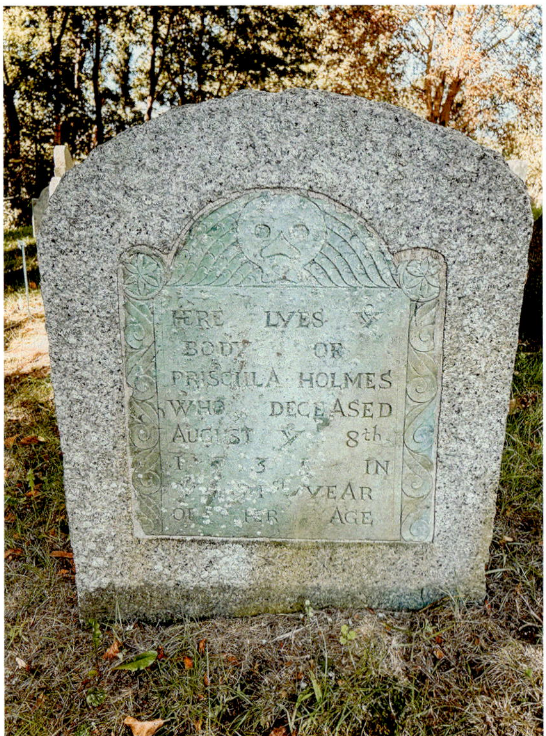

"Here lyes ye body of Priscilla Holmes, who deceased August ye 8th 1735 in the 21st year of her age."

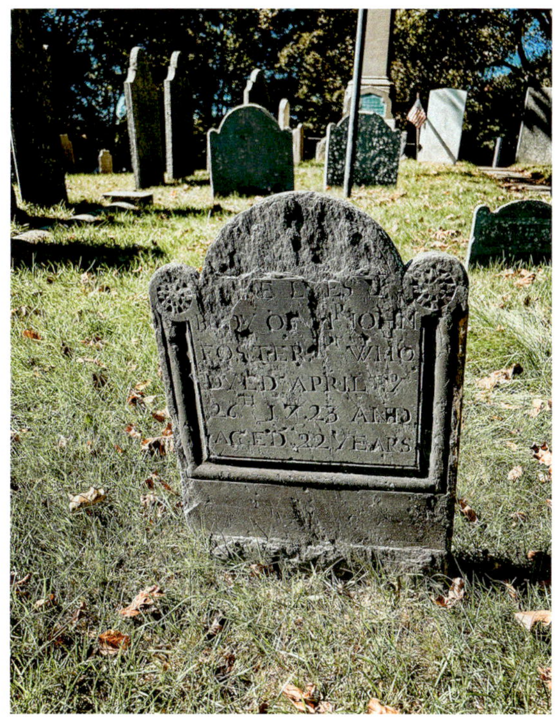

"Here lyes ye body of Mr. John Foster, who died April ye 26th 1723, aged 22 years."

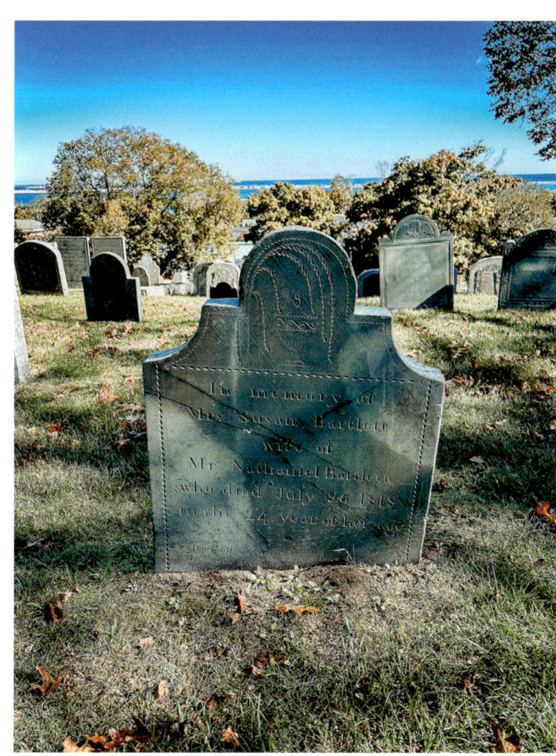

"In memory of Mrs. Susan Bartlet, wife of Mr. Nathaniel Bartlett, who died July 26 1818 in the 24 year of her age. Peace all our angery passions then let each rebellious sigh be silent at his Sovering will and every murmur die."

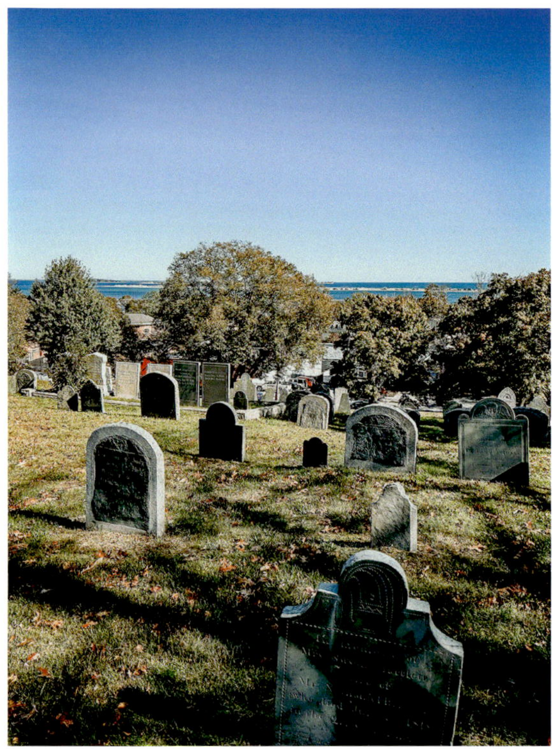

Here is another view of the grave of Mrs. Susan Bartlett, as well as some more of the hill and the bay.

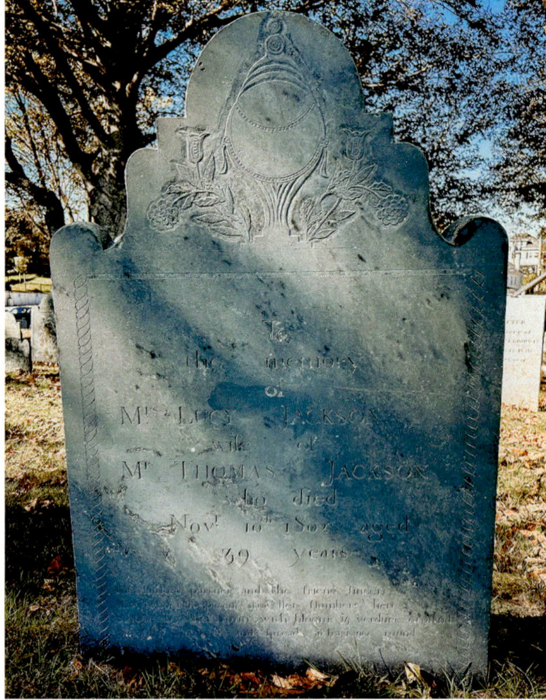

"To the memory of Mrs. Lucy Jackson, wife of Mr, Thomas Jackson, who died Novr 10th 1802, aged 39 years. The fainted partner and the friend sincere, the tenderest parent, traveller, slumbers here, smote by the storm with blooms and verdure crownd so falls the tree and spreads a fragrance round."

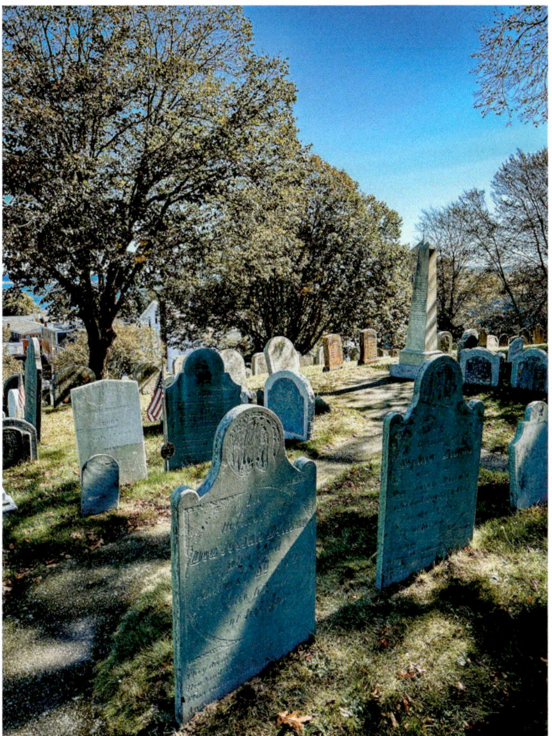

These graves in the front belong to Deacon Josiah Dimon and his second wife, Sophia. Sophia was the mother of three of his four children. His oldest son, Josiah Jr., died when he was seven days old on September 16, 1798, a little over a month before his mother, Susanna, died on October 24.

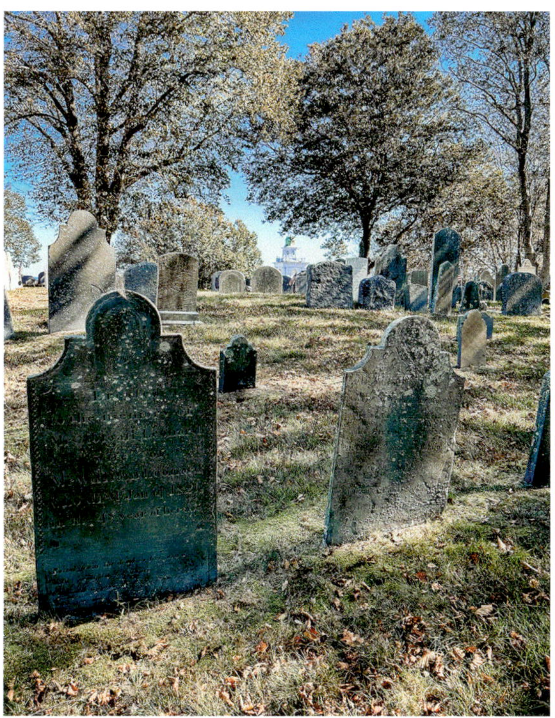

Mrs. Abigail Leonard died in 1821 when she was only forty-eight.

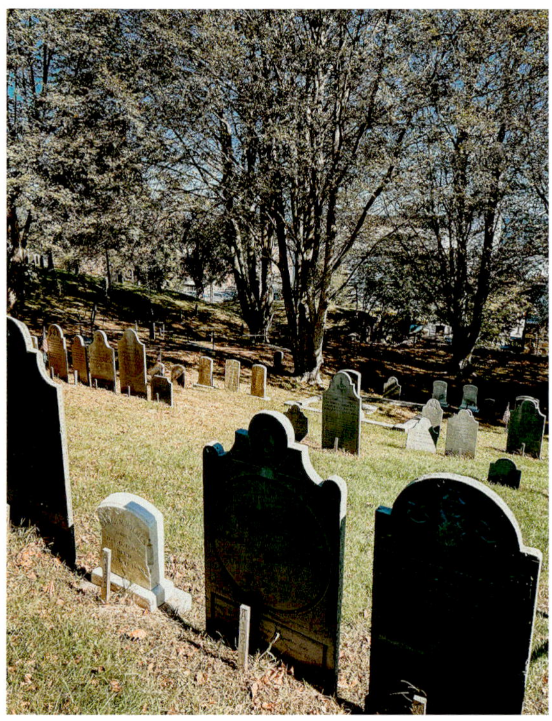

At the center of this photo is the grave of Eunice Holmes, aged forty. To her right is Eleanor Morton, also aged forty.

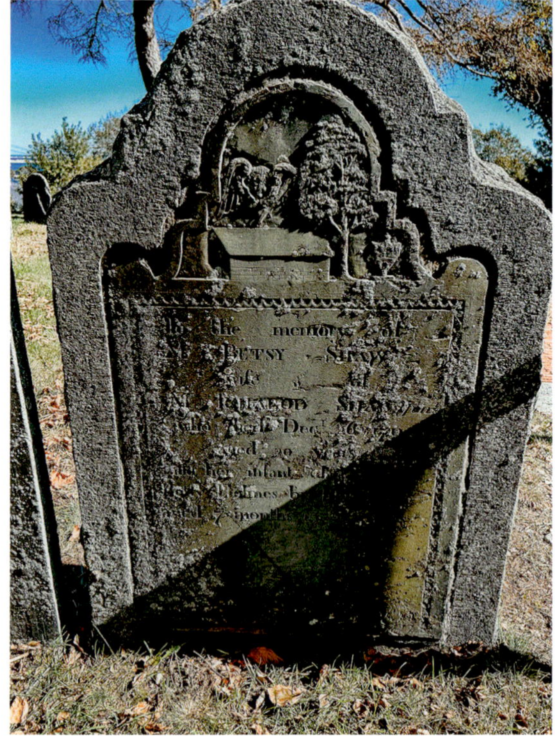

"To the memory of Mrs. Betsy Shaw, wife of Mr. Ichabod Shaw Jun.r, who died Dec.r 26, 1795, aged 20 years. Also, her infant daughter, Betsy Holmes by her side, aged 7 months and 15 days."

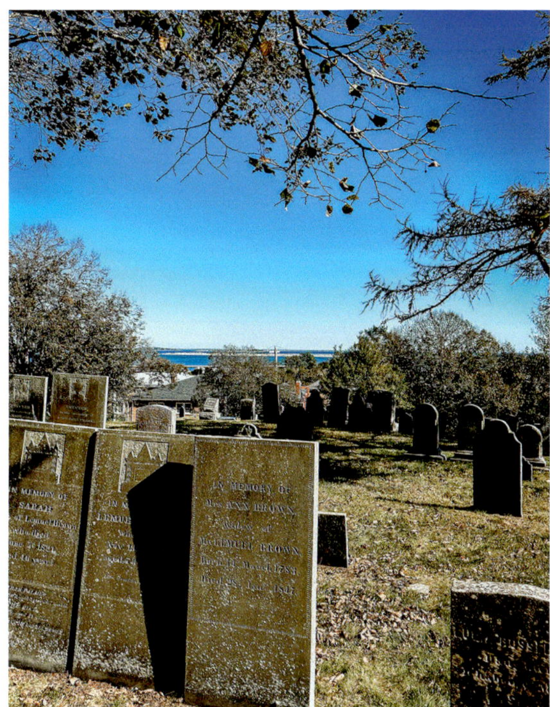

Here is another instance of a husband being buried with both of his wives. At the center of the three graves is Lemuel Brown. To his right is his first wife, Sarah; to his left is his second wife, Ann.

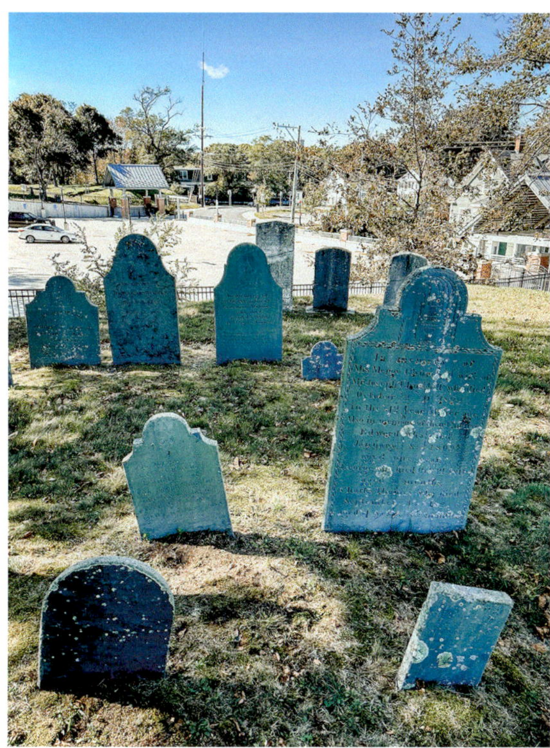

The small grave on the left belongs to Amelia Churchill, daughter of Joseph and Mercy, who died when she was seven months old. The grave on the right is in memory of Mercy as well as their sons, Edward, George and Charles.

Mercy died October 2, 1822, when she was forty-two. Joseph remarried Lydia Goodwin, Mercy's younger sister, October 19, 1823. They do not appear to have had children together.

Joseph died at sea, sailing from Boston to France on the *Plymouth Rock* in November 1836. His son Joseph would follow suit, dying at sea in August 1842. Lydia never remarried, living until she was eighty-one.

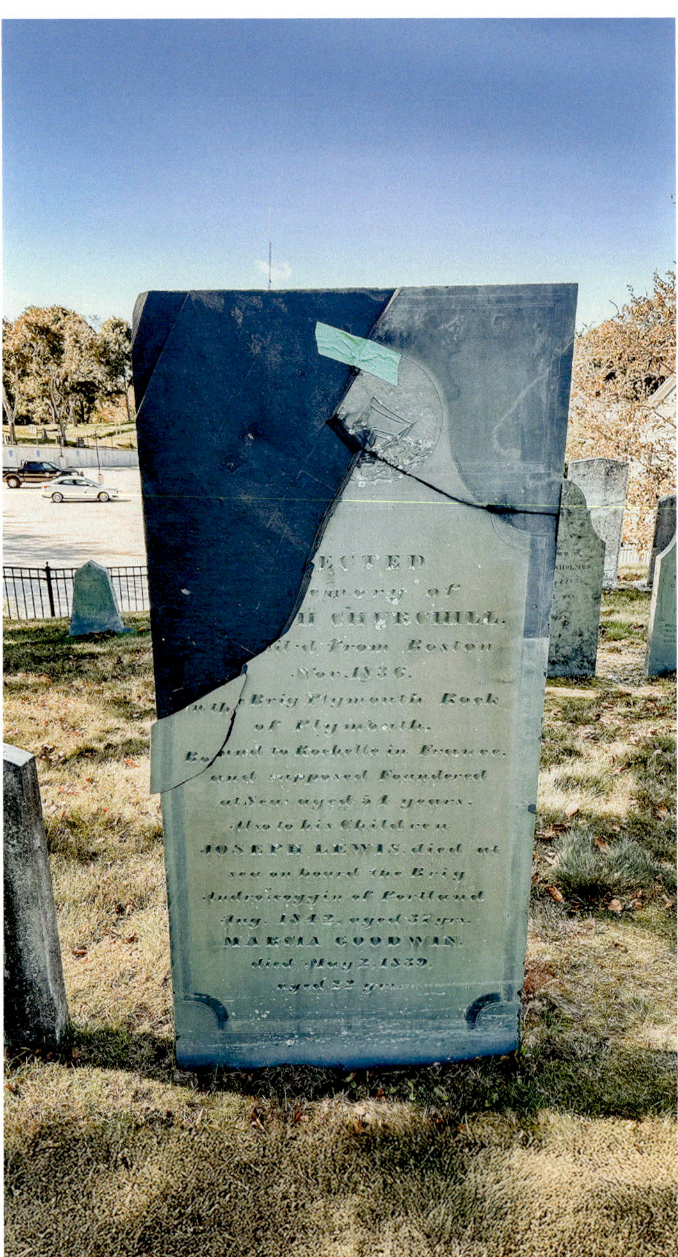

This broken grave that is attempting to be pieced back together belongs to three of the Churchills: Joseph and two of his children, Joseph Lewis and Marcia. Both father and son are not actually buried here though as they were lost at sea.

John Davie was born in Plymouth in 1809 to Ebenezer and Lydia; he was the fifth of eleven children. Priscilla Snow was also born in Plymouth, though she was born in 1819 to parents Leonard and Maria; she was the oldest of seven children. John and Priscilla wed on May 14, 1837. They had a son, John Jr., in 1838.

Priscilla died December 10, 1838, when she was only nineteen years old. John Jr. passed away a little over a month later on January 20, 1839, when he was only five months old; he is buried with his mother. After such a loss, it doesn't appear that John Sr. was ever able to remarry. He died only a few years later on June 27, 1841.

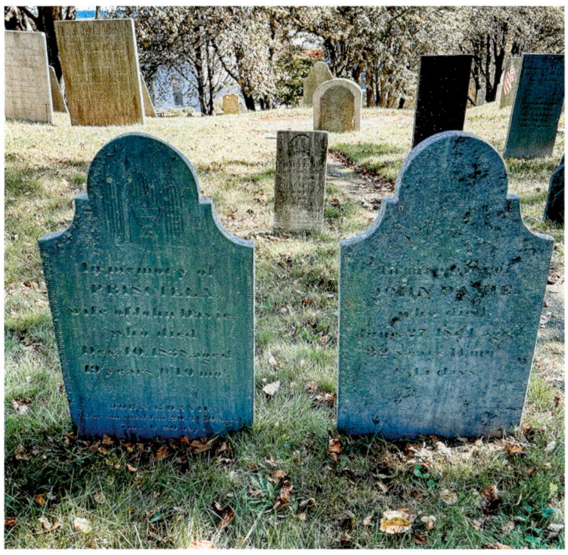

These graves belong to the Davies. To the left is Priscilla, along with son, John. Father and husband, John Sr., is buried to the right.

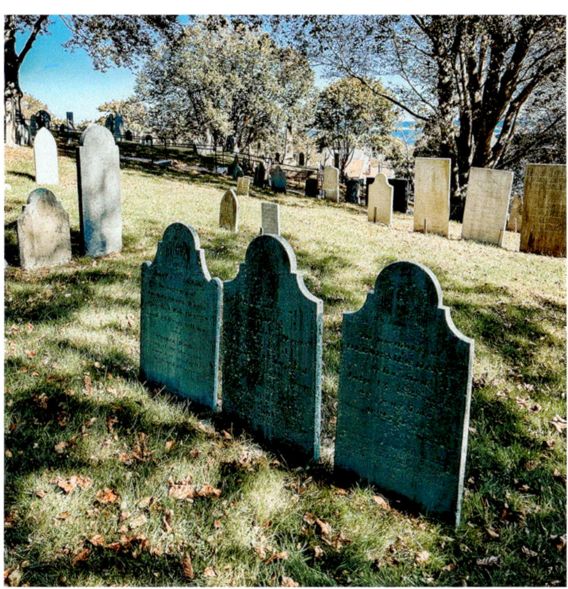

These graves belong to other members of the Davie family: Ebenezer and Lydia, parents to John, as well as Deborah, John's younger sister.

The Goddard family began when John Goddard married Mary Polden in Plymouth on August 8, 1756. They would have four children during their marriage: Mercy, Lydia, Mary (who went by Polly), and John. They lost all of their daughters young and many of the siblings never got to meet. Mercy died in 1762 when she was six years old. While the grave says she was six years old, I wonder if they meant "in her sixth year" like a lot of graves do in the area and she was actually five. For her to be six in August of 1762, she would have to have been born in August of 1756, which is when John and Mary got married. This would have been quite the scandal at the time.

Mercy died on August 10 while Lydia died on August 14; she was only two years old. Polly was born in 1765, but she died when she was two and a half on June 15, 1767. Their last child, their son John, was born in 1769, having never met any of his older sisters.

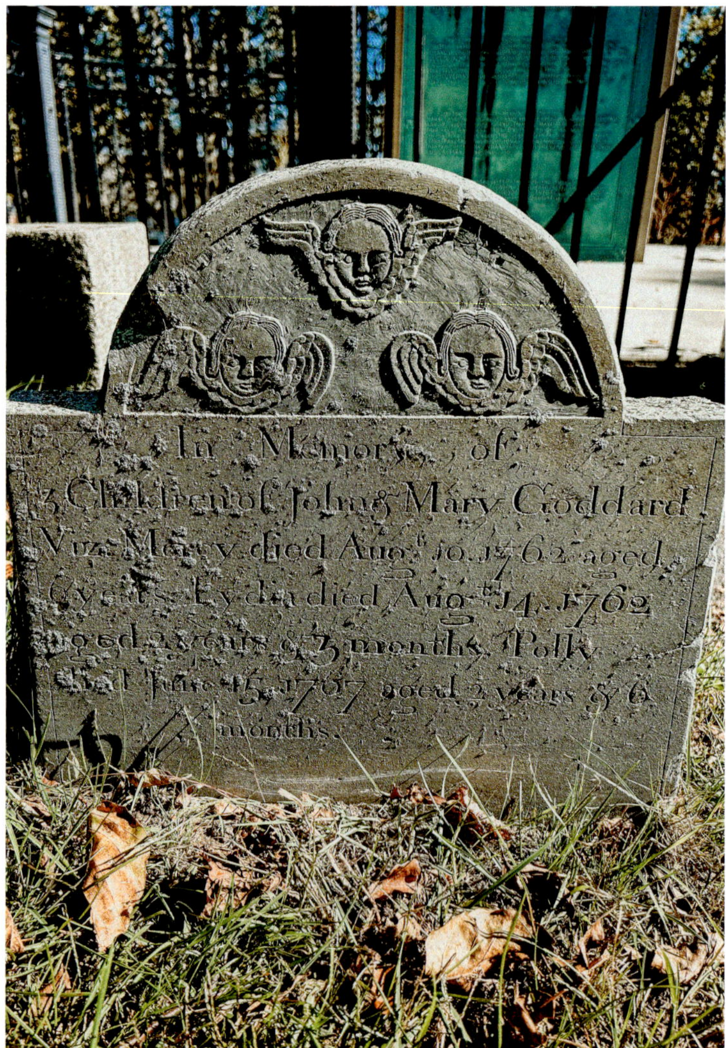

This grave belongs to three of the four Goddard children, complete with three winged faces representing their souls. Mercy and her younger sister, Lydia, both died August 1762, just four days apart. Lydia died five years later in June 1767.

Sarah Poor was born on August 20, 1776, to parents Daniel and Hannah as the sixth of eleven children. The sibling born directly before her was also named Sarah, but she died when she was eighteen months old in 1775. She would have four children with her husband, Reverend James Kendall, who she married on May 30, 1800. Their children were Sarah, James Augustus, Lydia, and Elizabeth.

Elizabeth was born on December 1, 1808, but would only live for thirteen days. She is buried with her mother who died about two months later on February 13, 1809. With mother and child both dying that winter it very well could have been disease, but with how close it was to Elizabeth's birth, I wonder if it was something to do with that; perhaps it was a difficult labor and Sarah never recovered. Regardless, tragedy would strike the Kendall family again just a year later when Lydia died on March 10, 1810, when she was only three.

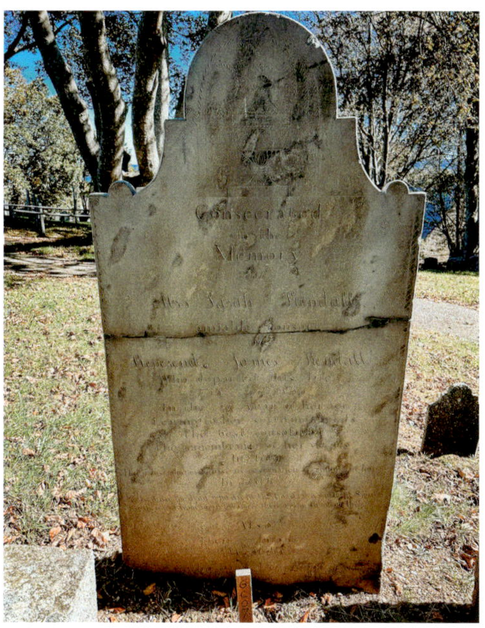

The grave of Sarah Kendall and her daughter, Elizabeth, was snapped nearly in half, but has been repaired. "Leaving to her surviving friends the best consolation, the remembrance of her virtues in life; her pious calmness, Christian resignation & triumphant hope in death." And for Elizabeth, "It is not the will of your Father which is in heaven that one of these little ones should perish."

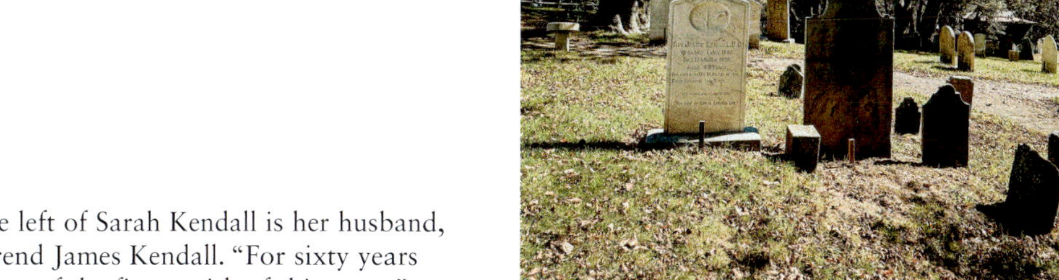

To the left of Sarah Kendall is her husband, Reverend James Kendall. "For sixty years minister of the first parish of this town."

Pamelia Dunham was born in 1783, marrying Samuel Robbins on March 8, 1800, when she was seventeen years old. They had ten children over the course of their marriage: Sally, Edward, Samuel, Ann, Pamelia, Josiah, Horatio, Adoniram, Daniel, and Lewis. She is buried with three of her sons who did not make it out of infancy; Edward who lived to five months, Adoniram who died at six months, and Lewis who lived to be eleven months. Pamelia herself died at age fifty in 1833, leaving Samuel with seven children. He remarried in 1834 to Hannah Churchill.

Elizabeth Nichols was born in Charleston, SC, on February 28, 1798, to parents George and Margaret. She married Frederick Freeman in North Carolina on December 27, 1821. While married in North Carolina, they moved to Massachusetts at some point as that's where all their children were born. They had six in total: Elizabeth, Frederick (1825–1827), Margaret, Frederick (1828), Otis, and Sarah.

Sarah was born in March of 1833 and that would be her mother's last act; it's noted on a family tree that Elizabeth died in childbirth on March 12 when she was thirty-five. Frederick would marry two more times; in a strange coincidence, his second wife, Hannah, died when she was thirty-five as well in 1838, about four years after they married. Their daughter, also named Hannah, died in 1838 when she was only six months old. He and his third wife, Isabella, never had children.

Lois Holmes was the first child of seven to parents John and Lois; she was born in 1734. While she was the oldest of seven children, she only got to meet one of her siblings in her lifetime. Her younger sister, Mercy, was born on August 9, 1736; Lois died on September 11 of that year. The Holmes family went on to have another daughter named Lois in 1744, the first daughter to be born after Mercy.

In Hannah Dyer's short life, she experienced immense tragedy.

She was born to parents Josiah and Hannah Cotton on April 3, 1709. She was the oldest of twelve siblings. While the first five Cotton children survived childhood, the same cannot be said for the younger seven. Hannah's younger brother, Josiah, was born in 1719 when she was ten years old. They would lose him the following year. By this age, Hannah was old enough to understand what was happening. From 1721–1734 she would lose six more brothers: an unnamed infant boy twenty-five days old in May 1721; Edward, sixteen days old in July 1722; another Josiah, aged two months in October 1723; another Edward, who was also two months in June 1726; Rowland, aged fourteen days in August 1727; and another Rowland in 1734, aged two years.

All of this to say that Hannah went through a lot as a child and teenager, not to mention what she likely saw her parents go through. Even if it was more common at that time, it doesn't make it easier. And while the Cotton family lost seven sons, they would also lose Hannah before their youngest was born.

Hannah lived to be twenty-two, but in that time was married twice. She married Tomson Phillips on September 9, 1725, when she was sixteen. They do not appear to have had children, and on December 6, 1729, Tomson died at sea. On May 18, 1730, Hannah married again, this time to William Dyer. Their union would be short lived as Hannah died on October 27, 1731; they do not appear to have had children either. From what I can find, William never remarried and passed away in 1741.

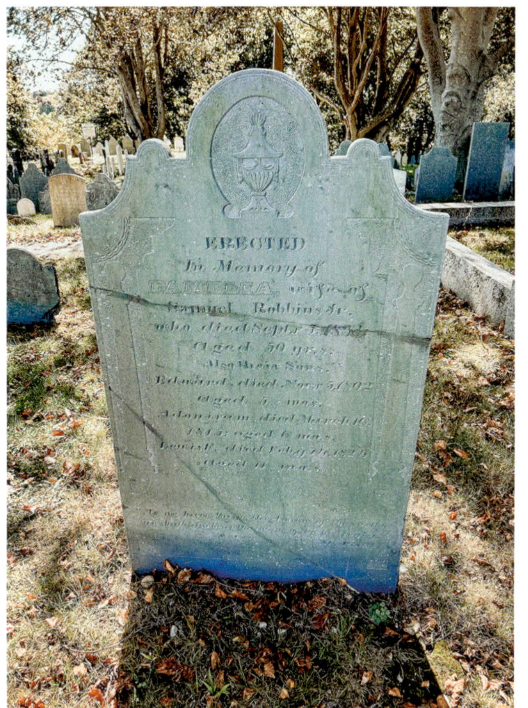

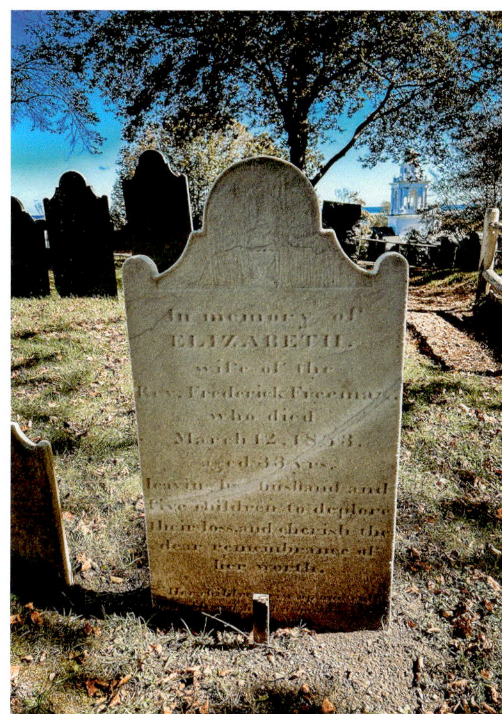

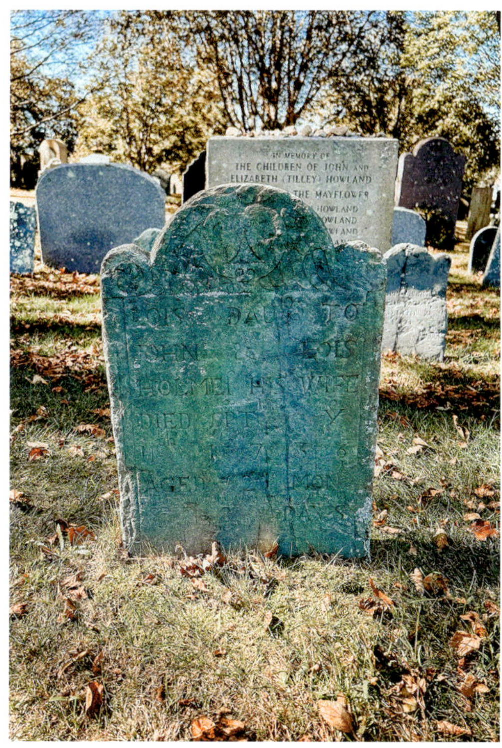

Above left: The grave of Pamelia Robbins and her sons shows two large cracks in it; photos online show where it was laying in pieces on the ground before being repaired.

Above right: "Leaving her husband and five children to deplore their loss and cherish the dear remembrance of her worth. Her children rise up and call her blessed; her husband also and he praiseth her."

Right: "Lois, dau'tr to John & Lois Holmes his wife. Died Sep ye 11th 1736, aged 20 mon & 8 days."

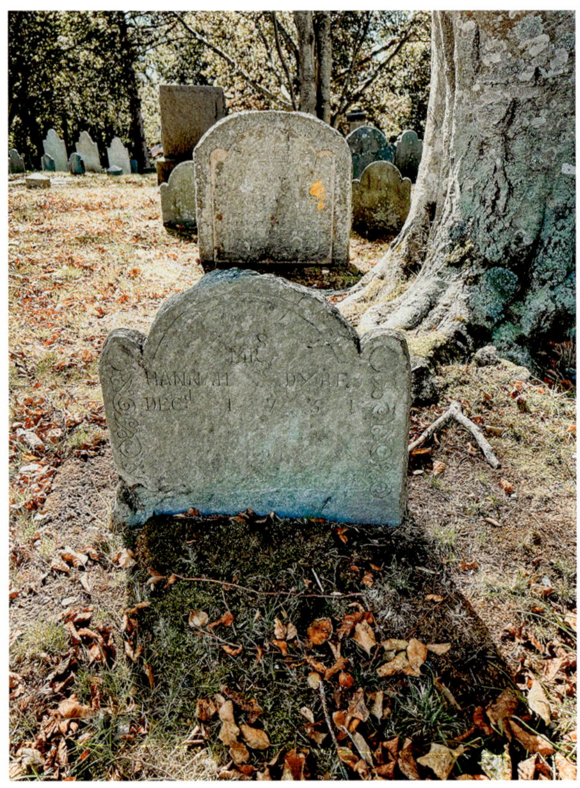

Pictured here is the footstone of Mrs. Hannah Dyer, though her last name is misspelled as "Dyre."

Josiah and Dorothy Carver were married on November 20, 1718. From 1722–1730 they would have six children, though only one would survive infancy. Josiah was born June 29, 1722, passing away on July 6 of that same year. They had an unnamed daughter who was likely stillborn as she was noted as being born and dying on April 29, 1723.

They had another son, Josiah, on September 25, 1724; he was the only one to survive to adulthood, living until 1799. He was married to Jerusha Carver and while they never had children, he was a stepfather to her son Edward from her first marriage.

January of 1730 was brutal for the Carver family. The year started with them losing their daughter, Dorothy, who was born May 20, 1727, on January 2 when she was just two years old. Their son, James, born May 5, 1729, died less than two weeks later on the fifteenth when he was only eight months old. While this is pure speculation, the loss of two children while she was pregnant likely caused Dorothy a lot of strain.

She went into labor on January 17 and gave birth to a daughter who would remain unnamed as she died that same day. This was very likely a premature birth, as James was only eight months old and pregnancies last (ideally) forty weeks or ten months. Dorothy died only three days later on January 20, most likely from complications from the early childbirth.

There are hardly any records on Josiah Sr. outside of when he married Dorothy, so it's hard to say if he remarried or ever had any more children. In the span of eighteen days, he lost his wife and three of his children, making his grief unimaginable.

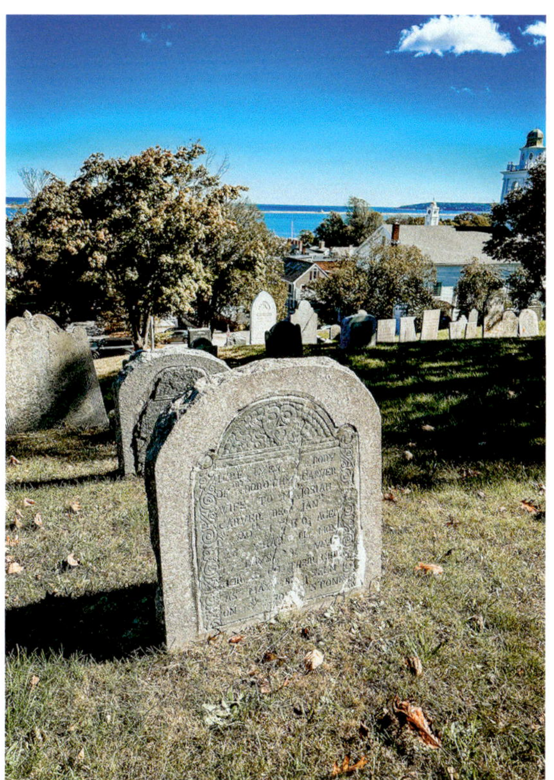

"Here lyes ye body of Mrs Dorothy Carver, wife to Mr. Josiah Carver, decd Janry ye 20th 1730-1, aged 28 years 11 Months 17 days, & near her 5 of their Chiln as may be seen on ye foot stone."

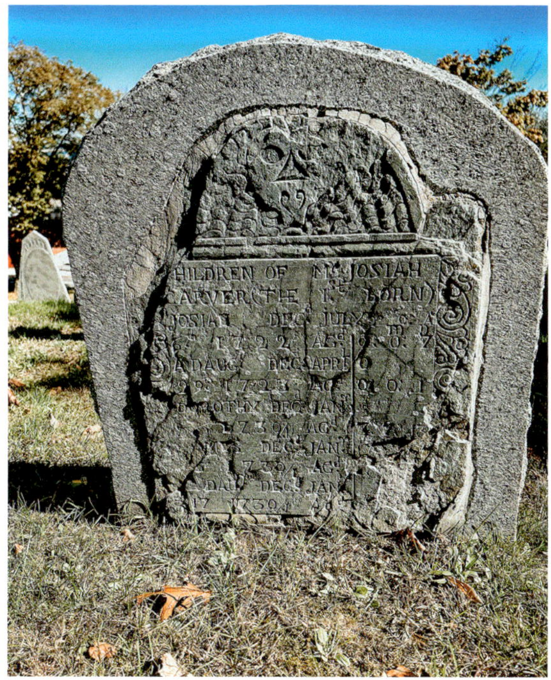

While their mother's grave has a vertical crack in the center, the gravestone of the Carver children looks to be in even worse shape, its crumbling making it difficult to read. "Children of Mr. Josiah Carver (the 1st born) Josiah decd July 6th 1722 Agd 7 Days, A daughr decd April 29th 1723 Agd 1 Day, Dorothy decd Janr 2d 1730 Agd 3 yr 7 mo 13 Days, James decd Janr 15 1730 Agd 1 yr 8 mon, A daur decd Janr 17 1730 Agd," and then it's broken off.

Patience Turner was born to parents Lothrop and Susanna in February 1801. She was the second youngest of five children to her parents; she also had an older half-sister from her father's first marriage. She was likely a welcome sight when she was born as her older brother, Eleazar, had just died in November 1800 when he was just one year old. Sadly, she was lost in November 1815 when she was only fifteen years old.

Deborah Lucas was born July 16, 1809 to parents Alden and Deborah. She was their first child and would be the oldest of five siblings: Deborah, Corban, Deborah, Charles, and Elizabeth. Tragically, she would never meet any of her siblings as she died July 24, 1810, when she was just over a year old. Corban, their next child, wasn't born until 1812.

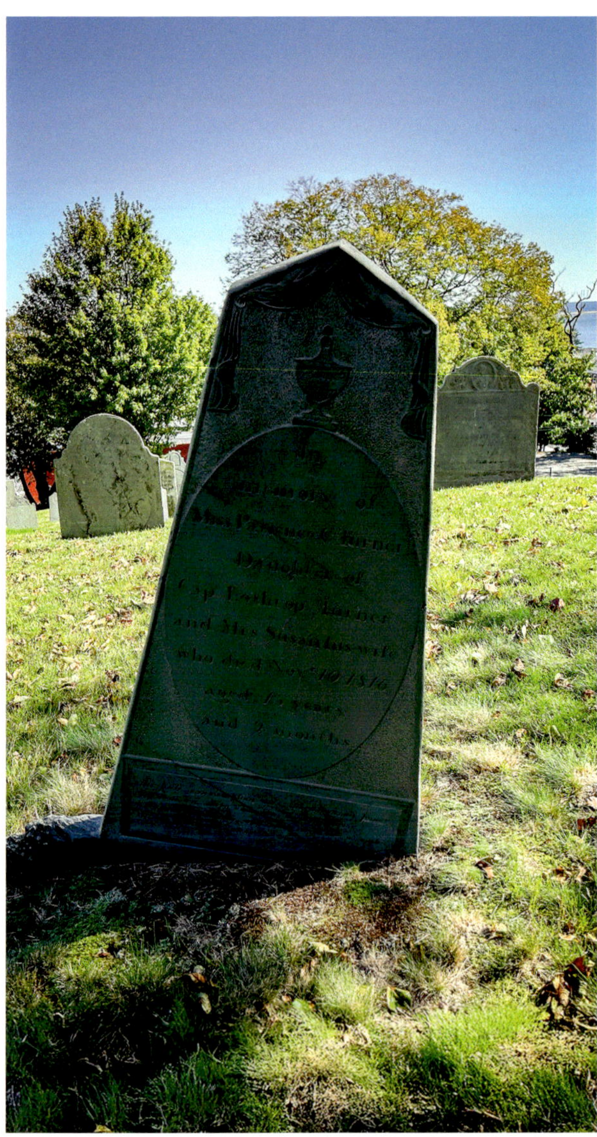

"In memory of Miss Patience Turner, daughter of Cap Lothrop Turner and Mrs. Susan, his wife, who died Nov 10, 1816, aged 15 years and 9 months."

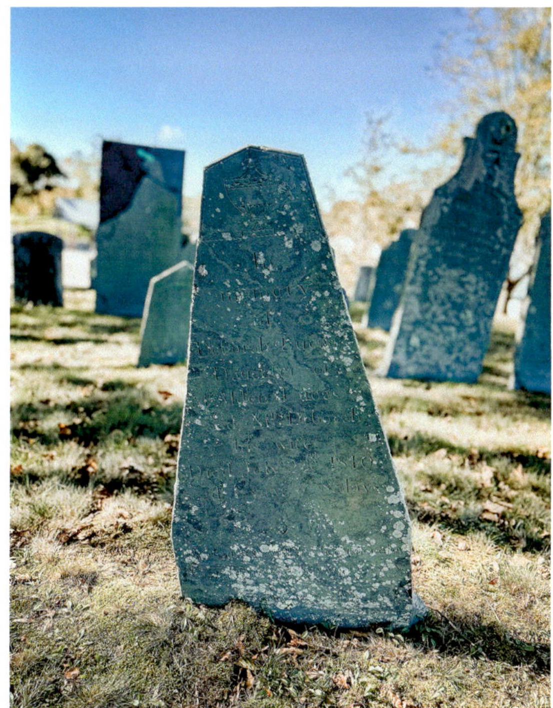

"In memory of Deborah Lucas, daughter of Mr. Alden Lucas and Mrs. Deborah, his wife. Died July 24, 1810 aged 1 year & 8 days."

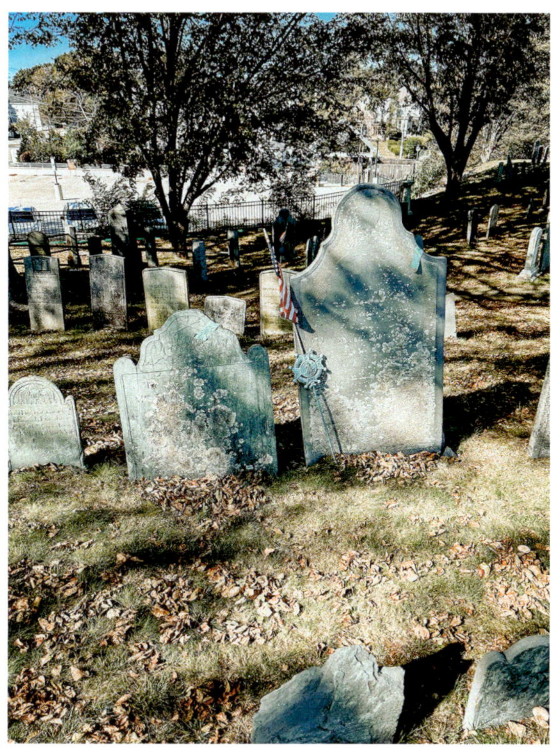

The small grave on the far left belongs to Hannah Goodwin. Her parents were Nathaniel and Molly; she died when she was just eight days old.

5

Unique Headstones

Thomas Russell doesn't have so much of a headstone as he does a boulder.

He was born September 25, 1825 to parents Thomas and Mary Ann. After graduating from Harvard and after practicing law for a few years, he became a judge when he was only twenty-seven. He eventually went on to the Superior Court of Boston for seven years. He held many positions over the course of his life including president of the Pilgrim Society, railroad commissioner, and he even served as minister to Venezuela under President Grant. Even though he was living in Boston when he died on February 9, 1887, his will instructed that he be buried in Plymouth. He died due to ongoing heart problems and a case of pneumonia.

James Warren is an important historical figure that I knew nothing about.

He was born in Plymouth on September 28, 1726, as a descendant of Richard Warren from the *Mayflower*; he passed away in Plymouth at the age of eighty-two in November 1808. Throughout his life, he held many important positions, many related to this country's independence. He was president of the Provincial Congress, a speaker for the House of Representatives in the General Court, and the paymaster general of the Continental Army; he held these positions at various times from 1775–1781.

In his personal life, he married Mercy Otis in 1754. Her brother, James Otis, is said to be the one to introduce the phrase, "Taxation without representation is tyranny." They had one son together named Winslow. Winslow was James's mother's (Penelope) maiden name. He was killed in 1791 in the Battle of the Wabash, which is also known as the Battle of a Thousand Slain during the Northwest Indian War.

Sarah Spooner's grave had two unique carvings, though only one survives today. Many of the headstones in the cemetery are now encased in cement in an attempt to preserve them. It can't be said for sure what happened to the bottom of the headstone, but it used to say, "Widow to" and then had a hand pointing towards her husband's grave. Remaining today is the carving of a Pilgrim woman at the top.

Sarah was born May 5, 1695, to parents John and Patience Nelson. Sarah was the second of four sisters: Lydia, Sarah, Abiel, and Hannah. I saw that Abiel is usually a male name, but marriage records confirm Abiel was another of the Nelson sisters.

Sarah would marry Thomas Spooner on December 12, 1717. They had four children together: Patience, Thomas, Sarah, and Ephraim. Sarah lived until January 25, 1767, when she was seventy-one years old.

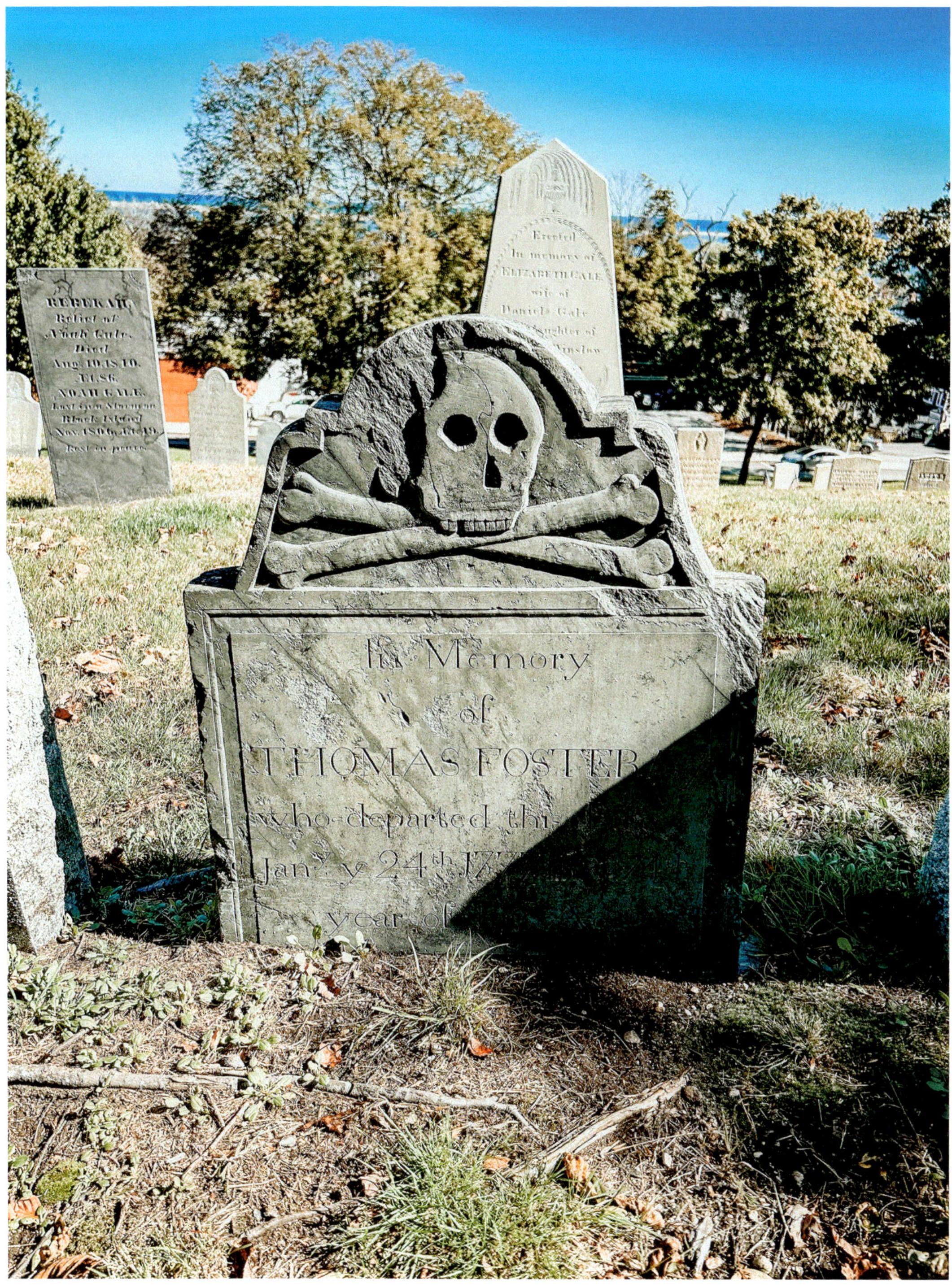

While many headstones have a skull and crossbones on it, Thomas Foster's caught my eye because it is so large and pronounced. Mr. Foster was born March 19, 1705, and died January 24, 1777.

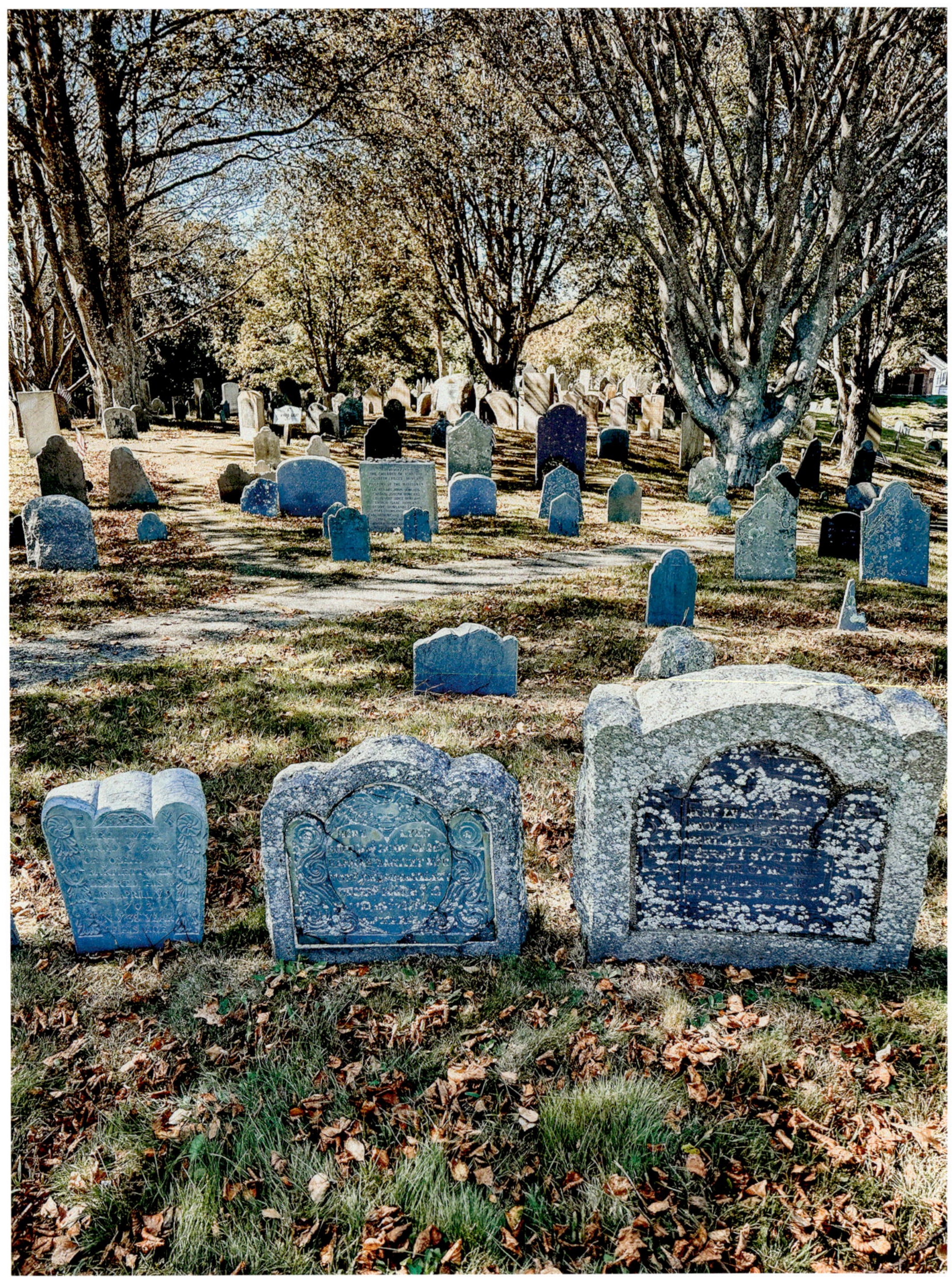

The grave of Mrs. Hannah Bartlett (center) has some beautiful carvings as well as a heart encircling her epitaph.

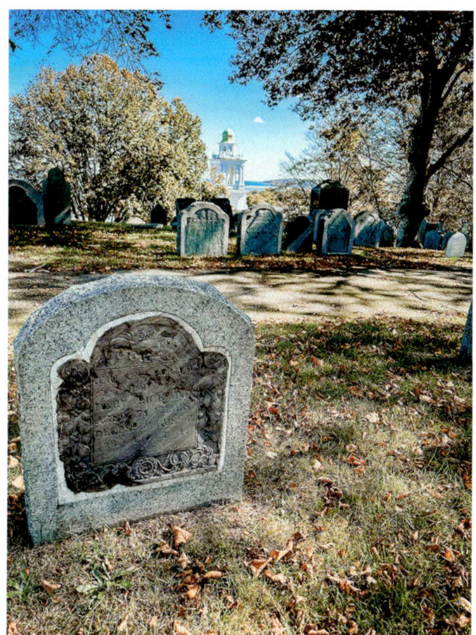

Right: The grave of Mary Rickard, fifty-five, has some beautiful detailing around the edges. It is now encased in stone to preserve it.

Below: The grave of Hannah Jackson (front left) has two winged faces as well as crossbones at the top.

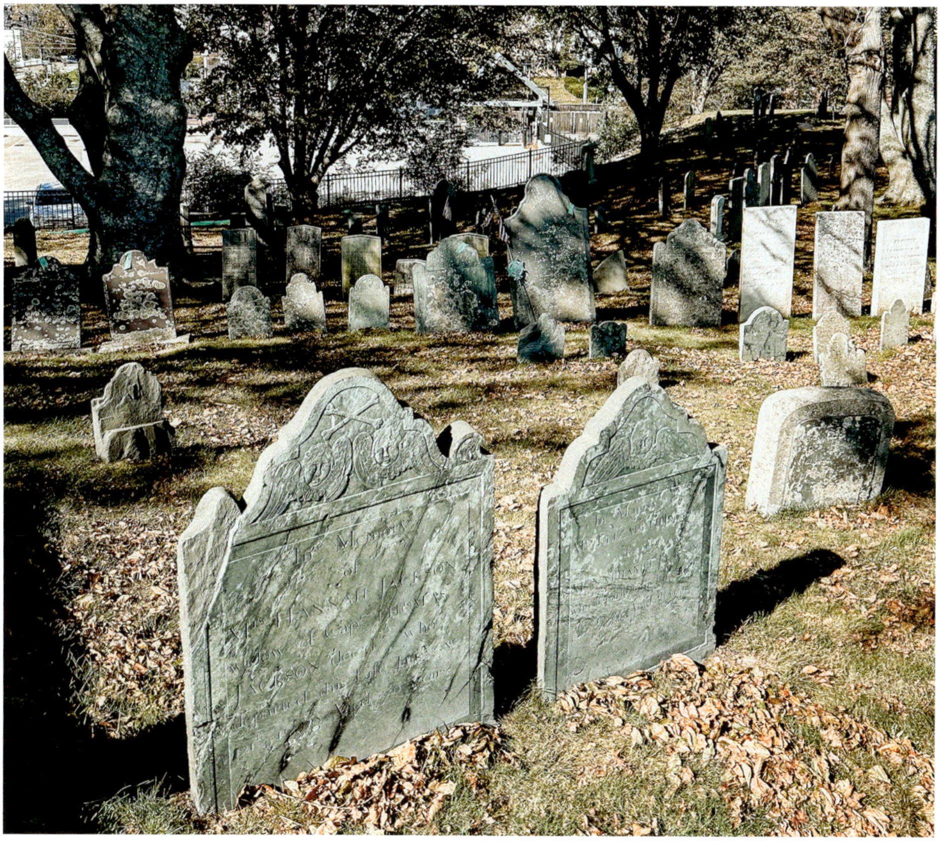

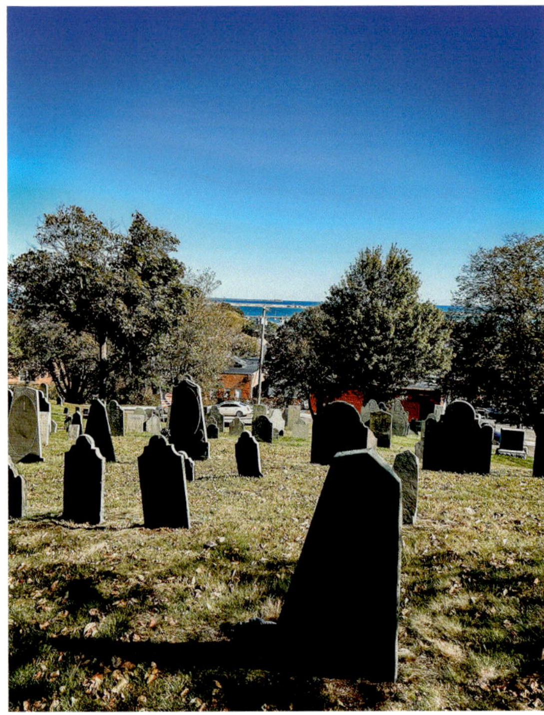

There are a few headstones that are pointed at the top rather than rounded, but they always catch my eye, nonetheless.

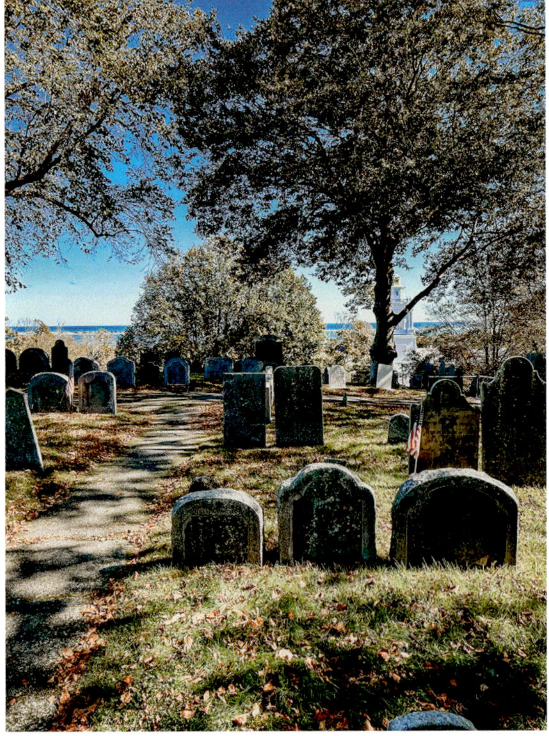

The practice of preserving the headstones within another stone may not seem unique as you are wandering around this cemetery, but I've yet to notice this practice in other older cemeteries I have visited through the Eastern U.S.

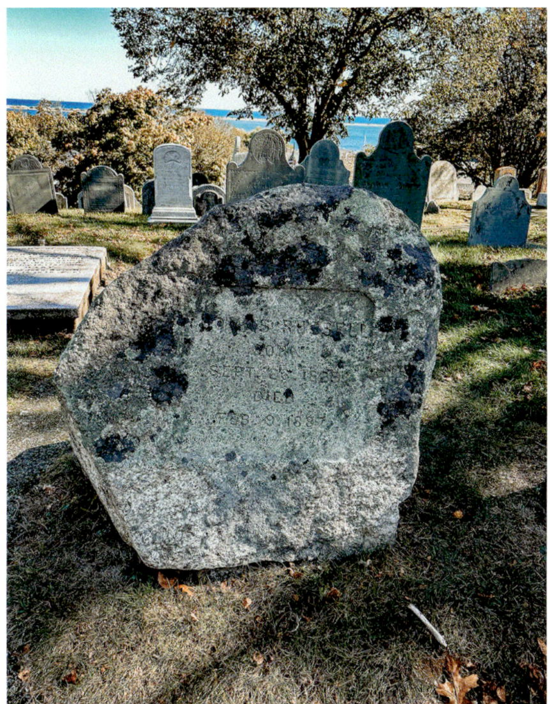

"On the top of this hill, not far from the monument of Governor Bradford, may be seen a granite boulder, brought from the pine hills of "Manomet," on which is neatly cut the following Inscription: THOMAS RUSSELL, BORN SEPT. 26, 1825, DIED, FEB, 9, 1887."

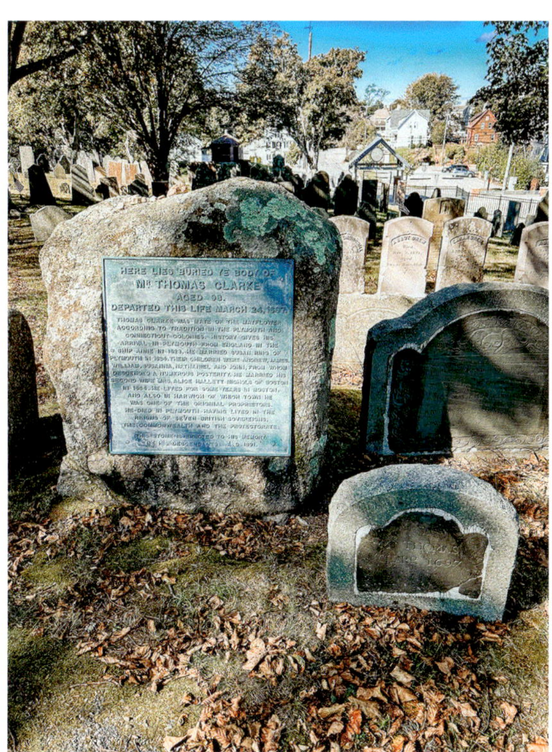

Thomas Russell isn't the only one with a massive tombstone. Thomas Clarke, who lived to be ninety-eight, is buried here.

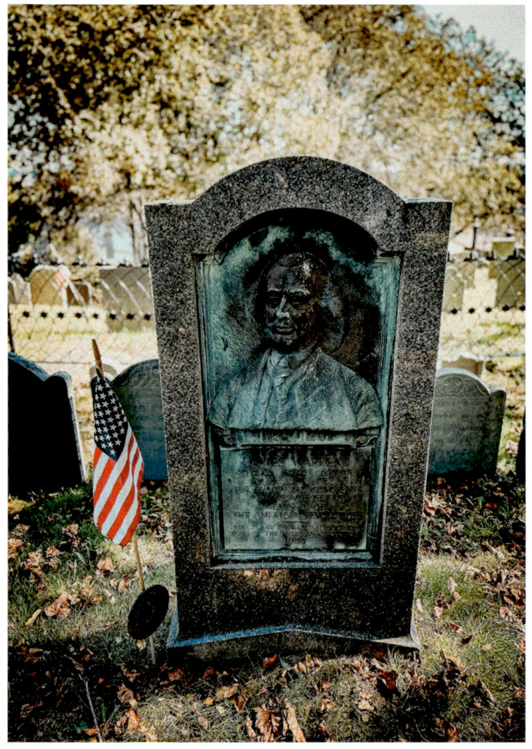

This is not the original headstone for James Warren; it was erected in 1928 by the Sons of the American Revolution.

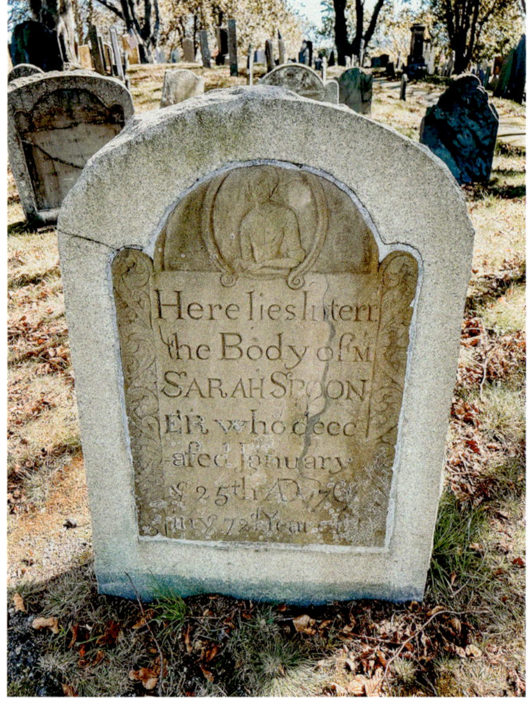

In addition to its unique carving at the top, you can see where they had trouble fitting the text onto the stone in several places. Her last name is broken up as "Spoon-er" and "dece-ased" is broken up as well.

The most intricate grave that I have come across is that of Nathaniel Jackson.

He was born to Abraham and Remember in January of 1664. He would marry Ruth Jenney on December 20, 1686, and they would have six children together: Nathaniel, Joseph, Samuel, Ann, Ruth, and Thomas. Nathaniel lived to seventy-nine, dying on July 14, 1743.

His headstone contains several distinct carvings, each with their own meanings. At the center is a skeleton with a scythe, meant to either be Death or Father Time. There is an hourglass sitting on the tomb where the skeleton is leaning; this is meant to show how quickly life passes. On the left side of the carving is a skull, which represents death or mortality. To the right is an urn that has a flame at the top, showcasing eternal friendship. The roses next to it have a few potential meanings.

Rose buds mean that the person died young, while a partial bloom means they were a teenager. A full bloom means the person died "in the prime of life," which could also potentially mean old age. Several buds are meant to show "secrecy." Nathaniel's contains a mix of buds and full bloom roses, so the intended meaning may be hard to figure. My best guess is the buds are meant for secrecy (of what though, I can't say) and then the full bloom roses were meant to show his old age.

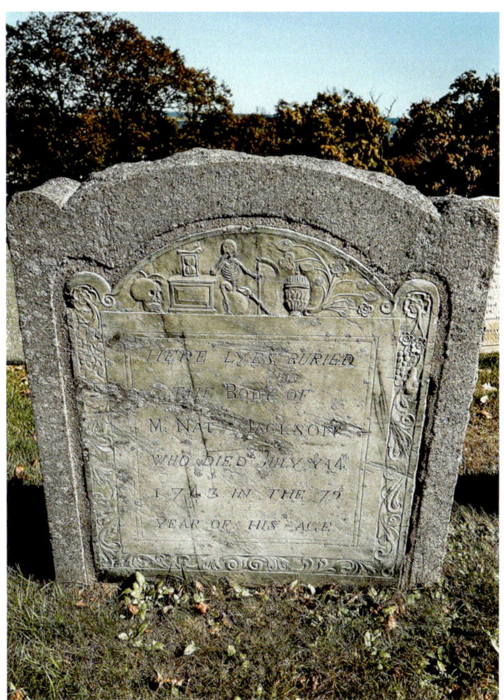

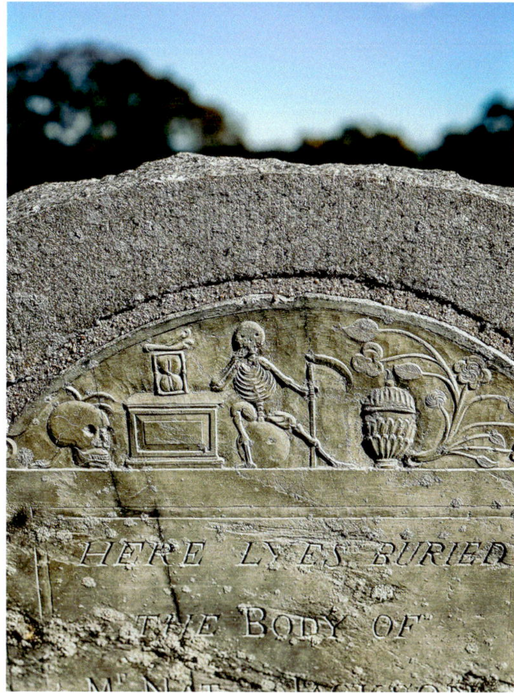

Above left: This is the grave of Nathaniel Jackson. Aside from the carvings, his epitaph reads, "Here lyes buried the body of Mr. Nat Jackson, who died July ye 14th 1743 in the 79th year of his age."

Above right: This photo focuses on the top of Mr. Jackson's grave and the intricate details.

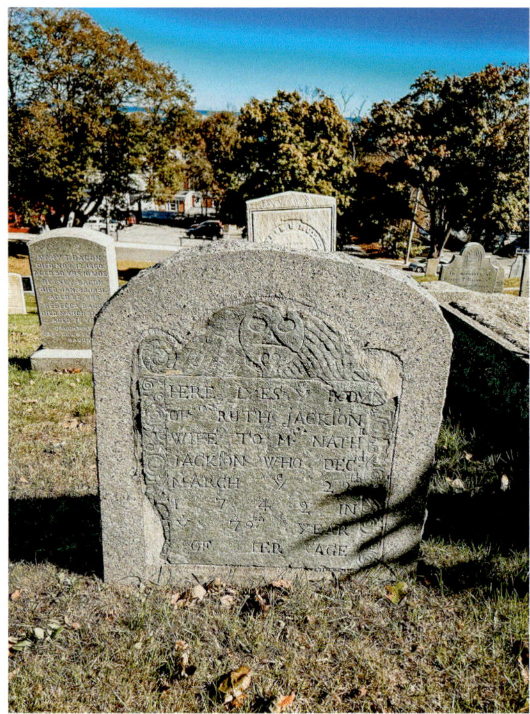

The grave of Mrs. Ruth Jackson is a bit more simplistic than that of her husband. Like many others, she has a winged face at the top which is meant to represent her soul. Ruth was born in 1663 and died March 29, 1742.

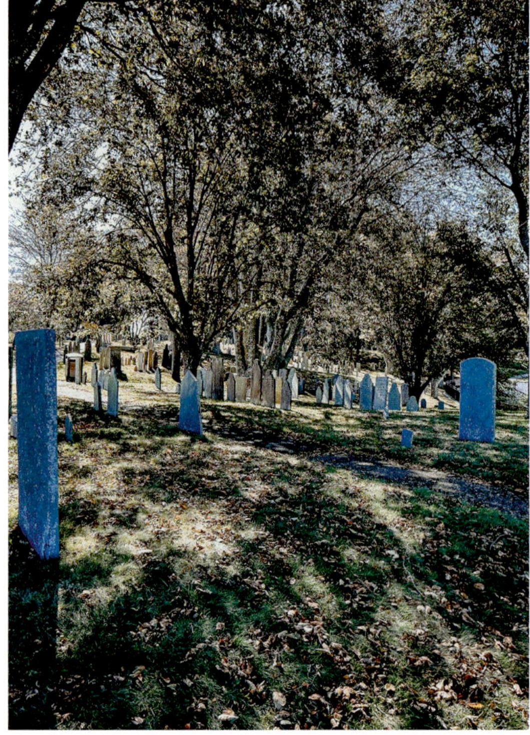

While there is no wrong time to visit Plymouth, fall is a particularly beautiful time of year, especially in the cemetery.

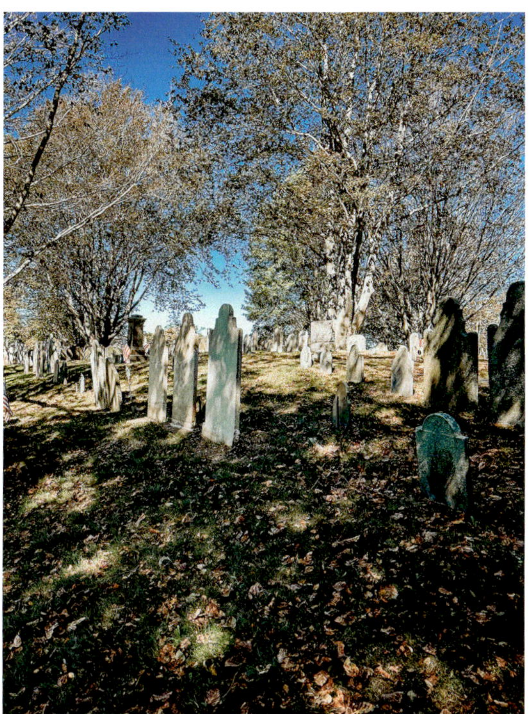

There is no time quite like fall in the Northeast, especially when you're visiting cemeteries.

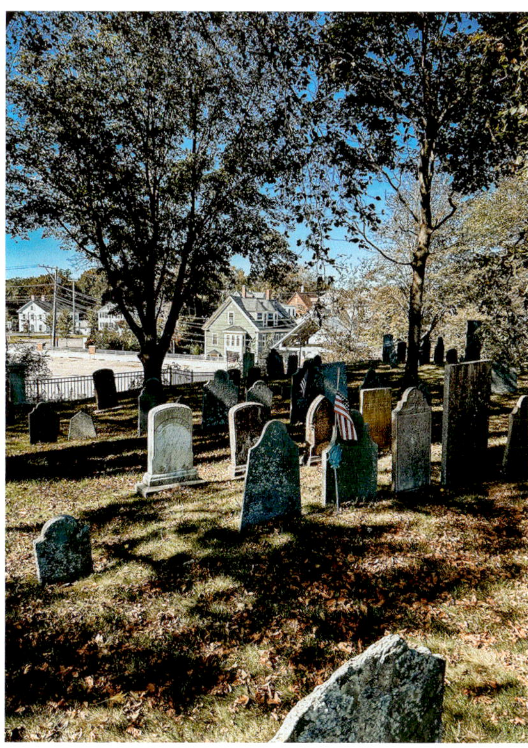

I always wonder what changes historical cemeteries have been witness to, especially one like this.

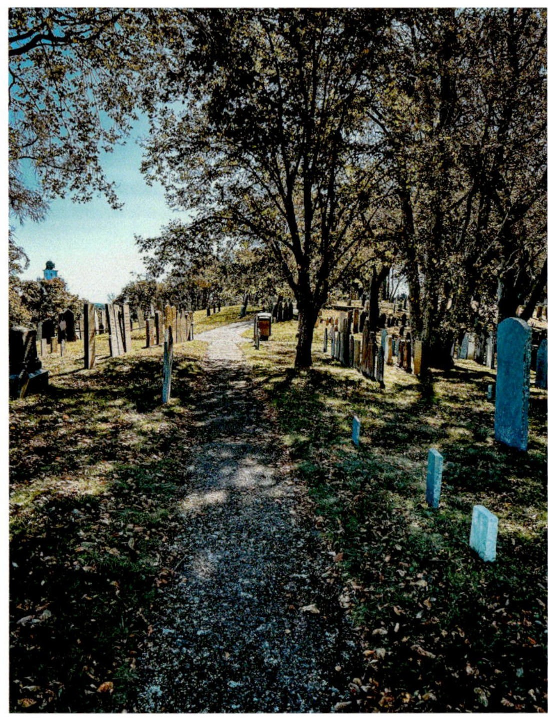

With its wealth of history and many pathways, it's easy to spend hours wandering in Burial Hill.

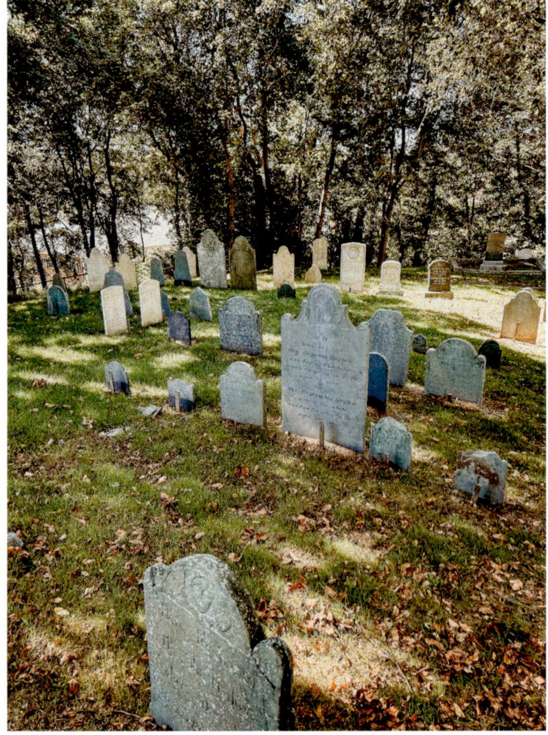

More graves in various conditions dot the landscape.

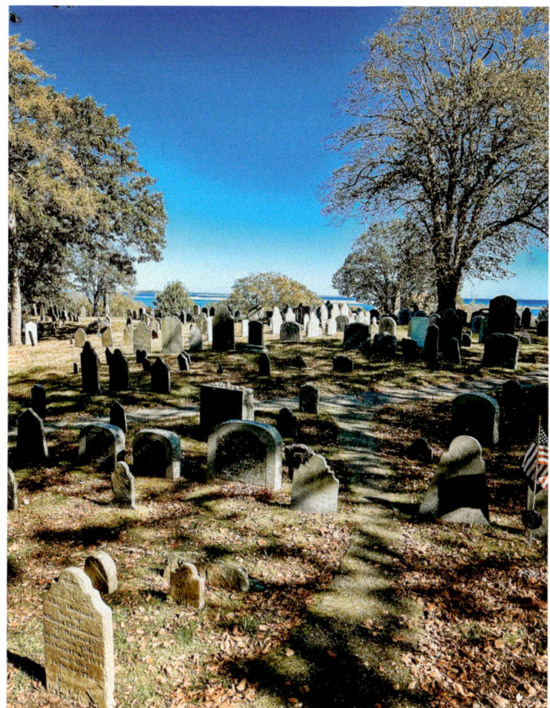

Before it was "Burial Hill," it was "Fort Hill." The fort as well as the original wooden grave markers are gone, leaving what stories we can find etched in stone. It is important to preserve this history while we can.

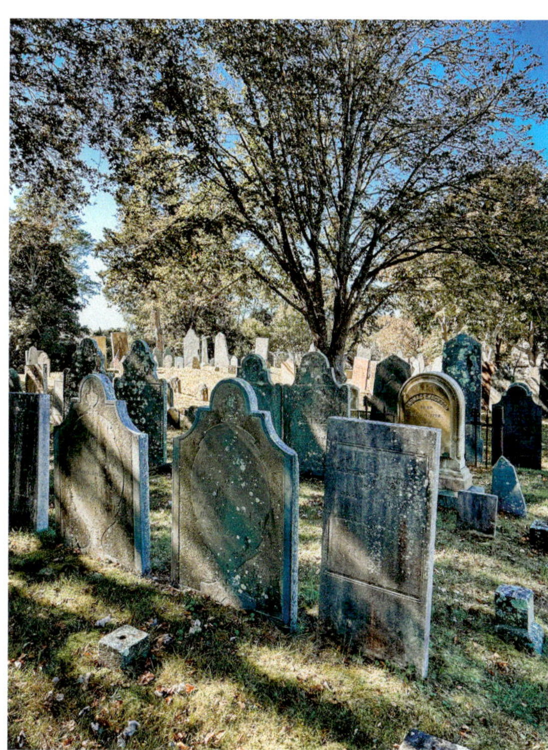

The last burials at the cemetery took place in the 1950s, but use of the cemetery had been declining for about 100 years as newer cemeteries were established.

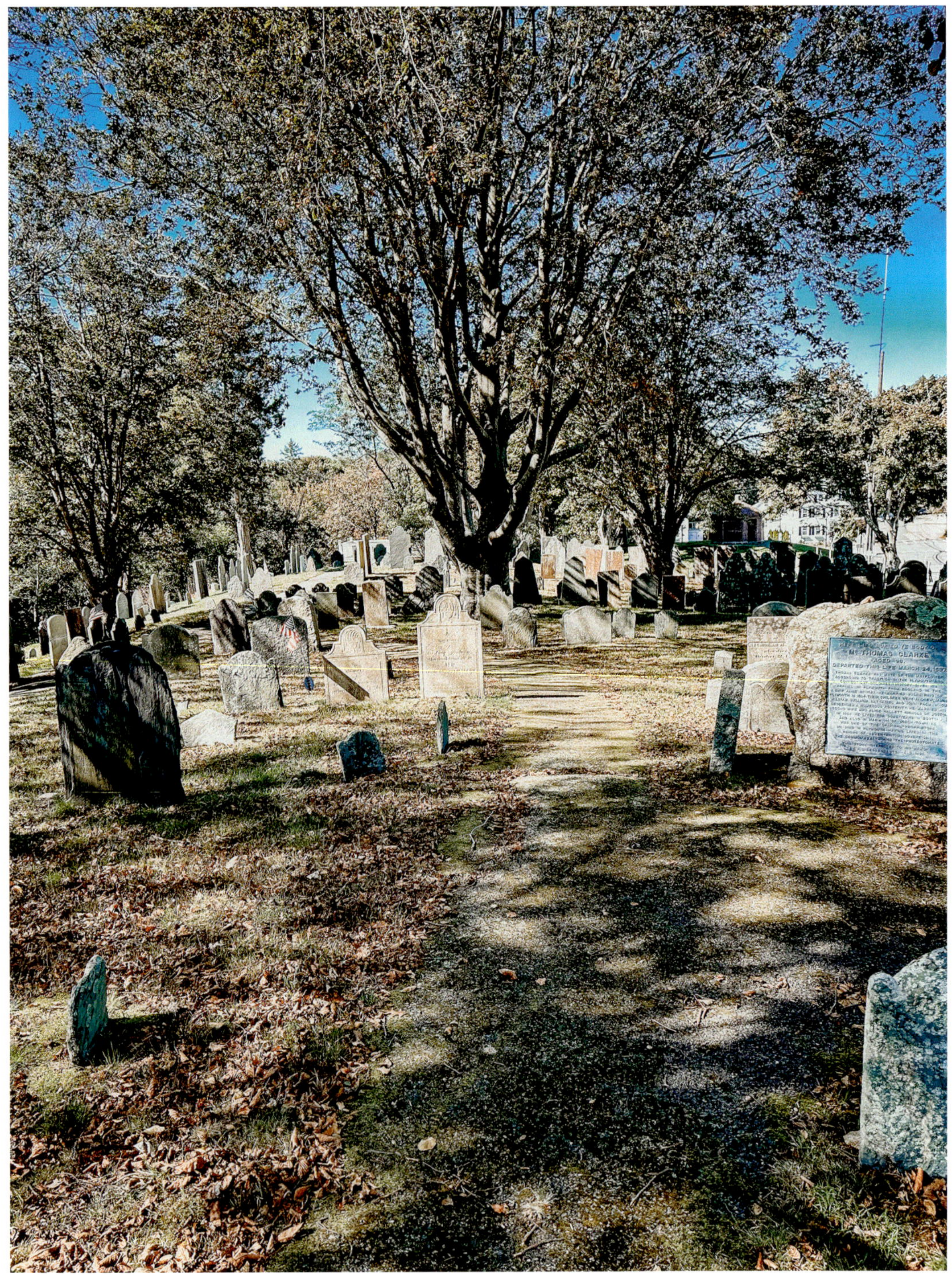

The winding and worn pathways of Burial Hill are some of my favorite photographs I've taken in a cemetery.

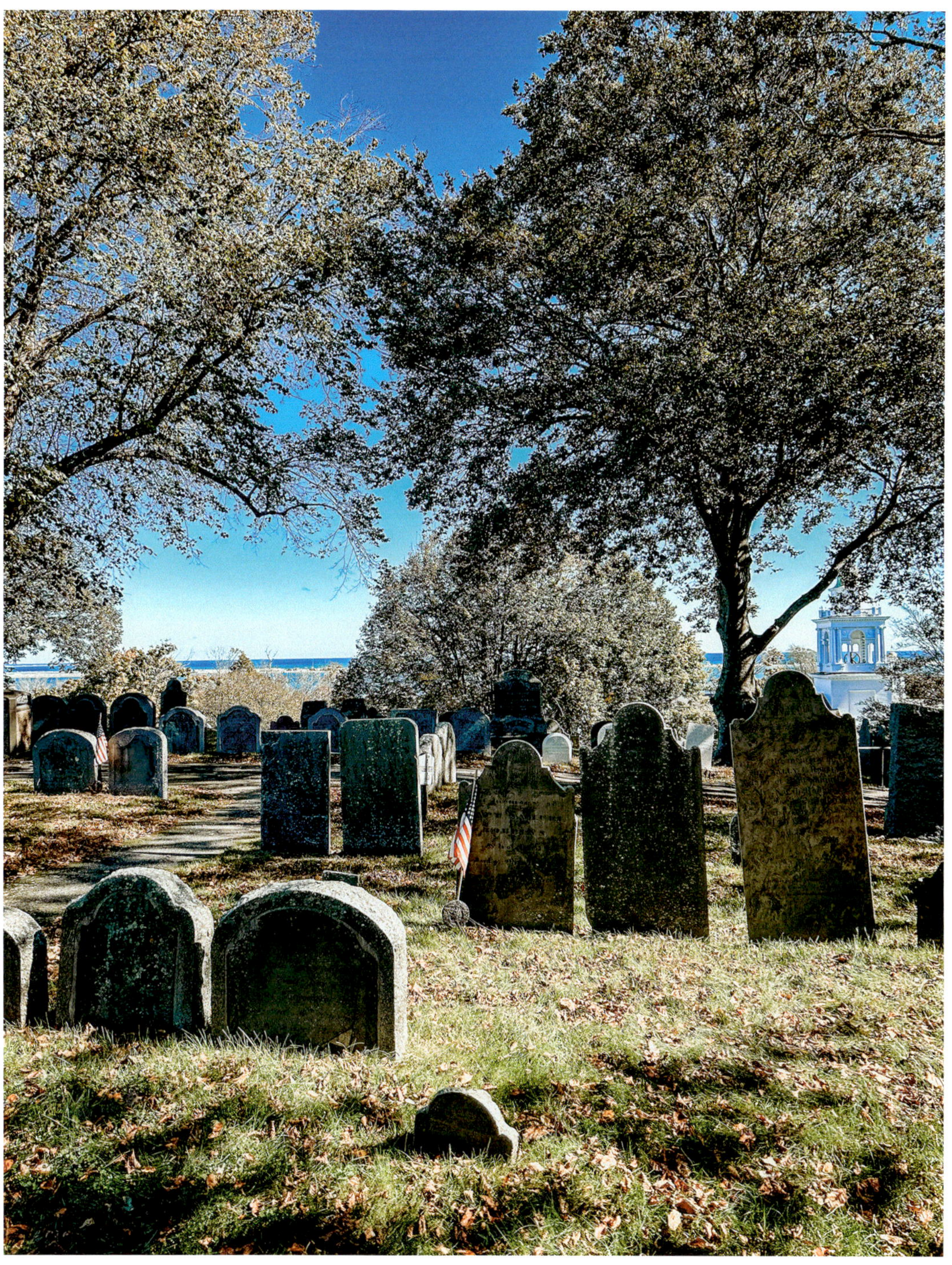

While researching I came across a quote, "You're not forgotten until someone doesn't say your name anymore." My goal is for the people who are buried here and whose stories have been shared are never forgotten.

$\mathscr{R}$EFERENCES

Family tree sources provided by findagrave.com, ancestry.com, Family Tree app and Geneanet community trees index.

1870 U.S. Federal Census
1880 U.S. Federal Census
Brooks, R. B., About Rebecca Beatrice Brooks. *Burial Hill Cemetery in Plymouth, mass.* History of Massachusetts Blog. https://historyofmassachusetts.org/burial-hill-plymouth/
Davis, W. T. (2012). *Genealogical Register of Plymouth Families.* Reprinted for Clearfield Co. by Genealogical Pub. Co.
Descendants of Francis LeBaron of Plymouth, Mass. Compiled by Mary LeBaron Stockwell Published Boston, Mass. by T.R. Marvin & Son, 1904
Gruber, Anya. "Burial Hill's Historic Gravestones Are Coming to Your Screen." *Atlas Obscura,* 8 May 2023, www.atlasobscura.com/articles/burial-hill-gravestones-digitized-archaeology
"Headstone Symbols and Meanings: A Guide to Cemetery Symbols." *Memorials.com Blog,* 18 Apr. 2022, www.memorials.com/info/headstone-symbols-meanings
Kristen. "Tragedy and Memory: The Wreck of the General Arnold." *Historical Notions,* 14 Feb. 2021, historicalnotions.substack.com/p/tragedy-and-memory-the-wreck-of-the.
Massachusetts, U.S., Compiled Marriages, 1633-1850
Massachusetts, U.S., Death Records, 1841-1915
Massachusetts, U.S., State Census, 1865
Massachusetts, U.S., Town and Vital Records, 1620-1988
Massachusetts, U.S., Vital Records, 1640-1849
Massachusetts, U.S., Wills and Probate Records, 1635-1992
Mayflower Births and Deaths, Vol. 1 & 2
Norbury Mackenzie, G., *Colonial Families of the USA, 1607-1775*
North America, Family Histories, 1500-2000
North Carolina, Marriage Records, 1741-2011
Port, Jane. *French Connections: New France & the Old Colony.* 2004
Ray, M. (2023). *James Otis & The Revolutionary War.* study.com

Russell Marble, A. (2016). *The Women Who Came in the Mayflower*. CreateSpace Independent Publishing Platform

U.S., New England Marriages Prior to 1700

U.S., Newspaper Extractions from the Northeast, 1704-1930

U.S. and Canada, Passenger and Immigration Lists Index, 1500s-1900s

ABOUT THE AUTHOR

Lexi has always had a love of all things dark and haunting, from true crime to ghost stories. Though she lives in Savannah, Plymouth has a special place in her heart. With a love for photography since she was young, Lexi has combined that with her love of spooky stories and travel for everyone to enjoy on her Instagram page @octoberallyear_. She began fully embracing her interests after becoming a mom as she wants her children to follow their passions, even if it makes them "weird."